The
Canary
Islander

Barrie Mahoney worked as a teacher and head teacher in the south west of England, and then became a school inspector in England and Wales. A new life and career as a newspaper reporter in Spain's Costa Blanca led to him launching and editing an English language newspaper in the Canary Islands. Barrie's books include novels in 'The Prior's Hill Chronicles' series, as well as books for expats in the 'Letters from the Atlantic' series, which give an amusing and reflective view of life abroad.

Barrie writes regular columns for newspapers and magazines in Spain, Portugal, Ireland, Australia, South Africa, Canada, UK and the USA. He also designs mobile apps and websites to promote the Canary Islands and expat life, and is often asked to contribute to radio programmes about expat life.

Visit the author's websites:

www.barriemahoney.com
www.thecanaryislander.com

Other books by Barrie Mahoney

Journeys & Jigsaws (The Canary Islander Publishing) 2013
ISBN: 978-0957544475 (Paperback and Kindle)

Threads and Threats (The Canary Islander Publishing) 2013
ISBN: 978-0992767105 (Paperback and Kindle)

Letters from the Atlantic (The Canary Islander Publishing) 2013
ISBN: 978-0992767136 (Paperback and Kindle)

Living the Dream (The Canary Islander Publishing) 2015
ISBN: 978-0992767198 (Paperback and Kindle)

Expat Survival (The Canary Islander Publishing) 2015
ISBN: 978-0992767167 (Paperback and Kindle)

Escape to the Sun (The Canary Islander Publishing) 2013
ISBN: 978-0957544444 (Paperback and Kindle)

Expat Voice (The Canary Islander Publishing) 2014
ISBN: 978-0992767174 (Paperback and Kindle)

Island in the Sun (The Canary Islander Publishing) 2015
ISBN: 978-0992767181 (Paperback and Kindle)

Message in a Bottle

Barrie Mahoney

The Canary Islander Publishing

ISBN 978-0995602700
www.barriemahoney.com

First Published in 2012
Second Edition 2016

The Canary Islander Publishing

Acknowledgements

I would like to thank all those people that I have met on my journey to where I am now.

To supportive friends who helped me to overcome the many problems and frustrations that I faced and taught me much about learning to adapt to a new culture. Also, to friends in the UK, or scattered around the world, who have kept in touch despite being so far away.

To the people that I met whilst working as a newspaper reporter and editor in Spain and the Canary Islands, and for the privilege of sharing their successes and challenges in life.

Disclaimer

This is a book about real people, real places and real events, but names of people and companies have been changed to avoid any embarrassment.

The
Canary
Islander

DEDICATION

This book is dedicated to expats all over the world who dream of a new life, new experiences, new cultures, new opportunities to experience, taste and smell the excitement of a place that is of their own choosing and not merely based upon an accident of birth.

Contents

Preface

The
Canary
Islander

Hopeful Messages

'Message in a Bottle' has little do with the tragic love letter discovered in a bottle on the beach, or that forlorn song about a castaway who sends out a message in a bottle to seek love, yet one year later has received no replies and senses that he is destined to be alone forever.

On the contrary, this 'Message in a Bottle' is intended to be a message of hope published as a direct response to messages received from many regular readers of my 'Letters from the Atlantic' blogs and previous books, who empathise with both the joys and frustrations of being an expat. It seems that messages from this small island in the Atlantic are being heard.

It is true that there are times when the expat feels very alone, and even more so when not living in an enclave of fellow countrymen. Confusion and misunderstandings about cultural and legal issues often abound when not speaking in one's native tongue.

The worldwide recession too has brought with it many negative changes and implications for expats, as governments desperately attempt to reduce their spending. It is often the expat who suffers from changes in health, social security, legal, housing and employment laws, which have been hastily prepared and implemented by foreign governments, with many ignoring their wider responsibilities to their expat citizens.

There is no doubt that life for the expat has become more difficult and more challenging in the last few years. The opportunities for leaving one country and settling in another is now less easy than it has been in earlier years.

Reduced employment opportunities, severe fiscal challenges, as well as a 'bringing the shutters' down policy in some countries has reduced the fluidity of movement of people between countries that we have seen in the previous three decades.

In addition, it is now less easy to gain and release unused equity in owner-occupier homes, which has previously funded second homes or a new life abroad. This was, of course, fuelled by rapid rises in house prices, which we now know was one of the factors behind the global economic crisis.

However, all new challenges bring with them new opportunities. I have met many expats who, after being faced with unemployment and what seemed like insurmountable problems in their home country, have quickly adapted to life in a new country.

Many have spotted a new business or career opportunity, discovered a dramatic reduction in personal stress, their health has improved, leading to a new found contentment and happiness.

This book is intended to bring a message of hope and reassurance to all would be and existing expats, as well as a reminder that many opportunities still and will always exist for the enthusiastic and open-minded expat, who can see beyond the horizon and the narrow confines of the country of birth.

History and Culture

The
Canary
Islander

A Queen Calls...

The launch of the new Cunard Queen Elizabeth caused considerable interest, not only in her new home port of Southampton, but also in Las Palmas de Gran Canaria, which was one of the first ports of call during this super liner's maiden voyage.

Appropriately, the Queen Elizabeth, which is the same length as 36 London buses and holds 2,092 passengers, started her maiden voyage on a 13-night cruise to the Canary Islands on 12 October 2010. This maiden voyage was fully booked within 29 minutes after it went on sale, and more than 50% of its remaining 2010 cruises were sold within one and a half hours.

Little was been made in the press that the official launch of the new liner by Queen Elizabeth took place on 11 October and the maiden voyage to the Canary Islands started on 12 October - Columbus Day. The day itself always causes some dispute each year, because Columbus Day in Spain is always celebrated on 12 October. However, in the United States, Columbus Day is always celebrated on the second Monday in October, which in 2010 was 11 October.

It was not the first time that a vessel of intrigue, excitement and anticipation had docked in Gran Canaria's famous port of Las Palmas...

Back in 1485, Portugal refused funding to Christopher Columbus. It took him seven years of lobbying to get funding from Ferdinand and Isabella of Spain. Initially, Queen Isabella turned him down and sent him away.

Later, King Ferdinand called him back and granted the funding. Half the financial support also came from private Italian investors. Columbus set sail and made it to the Canary Islands in August 1492.

Columbus arrived in Gran Canaria's port of Las Palmas, where he restocked the provisions and made repairs, and on September 6, started what turned out to be a five-week voyage across the Atlantic Ocean.

The five-week voyage across the Atlantic by Columbus actually started from La Gomera, one of the smaller of the Canary Islands. La Gomera has a fascinating association with Christopher Columbus.

Popular legend, speculation and contemporary reports all indicate that Columbus was in love with one of its most infamous of residents, the aristocratic Beatriz de Bobadilla, by reputation a vicious medieval nymphomaniac, and by all accounts, a great beauty.

Having said goodbye to his beloved, Columbus sailed for five weeks before land was sighted on October 12, 1492 and Columbus called the island (in what is now the Bahamas) San Salvador, although he continued to believe he had reached Asia until his death in 1506. He also believed the peaks of Cuba to be the Himalayas, which says little for his sense of direction!

Columbus Day has been celebrated as a holiday in Spain since 1958, as 'Día de la Hispanidad'. Well, it is an excuse for another fiesta!

Size Does Matter

It is rare to see Americans visiting these islands nowadays, which is probably due to the long flight and some similarity to the Caribbean Islands.

However, until the horrors of September 11, many tourists from the USA visited the Canary Islands regularly. Concerns about long air flights and security meant that flights from the USA were more or less halted and, until recently, these islands have seen a much-reduced number of visitors from the other side of the Atlantic.

This state of affairs is about to change once again with recent meetings between the President of the Canary Islands and the American Government with a view to extending and developing business links to these islands. After all, the Canary Islands are situated in an ideal strategic position for easy access to all parts of the European Community, as well as Africa and Asia and recent improvements to telecommunications have opened up considerable trading and business opportunities.

Trade and business links aside, these islands mean a great deal to many American citizens, many of whom have ancestry firmly based in the Canary Islands.

This fascinating story begins in 1778 in Louisiana, then a Spanish colony, when 700 men were recruited to increase the size of the Louisiana Regiment. The Spanish Crown had held Louisiana since 1762, and the possibility of an invasion by Great Britain was becoming a worrying threat.

Spain looked to the Canary Islands for recruits to increase the size of the army in Louisiana. Despite initial attempts to recruit single men, there were insufficient volunteers. Finally, the Spanish Government had to settle for married recruits with the dual role of defending the territory, as well as populating it. After all, as history tells us, there is more than one way to win a war and colonise a territory than using guns alone.

The new recruits from the Canary Islands had to be aged between "17 to 36 years old, healthy, without vices, and more than five feet tall". Recruiters were paid extra for every half-inch that each recruit stood in height above the minimum of five feet specified, so size was an important factor in their selection. These men were recruited on the understanding that they would be staying in Louisiana permanently, although there was no written agreement.

By the summer of 1779, 352 families and 100 single men had arrived in Louisiana, where the Governor, Bernardo de Galvez, settled them in four areas that he considered to be major invasion routes planned by the enemy. The men were formed into militia units led by Galvez in his conquest and occupation of British territory on the lower Mississippi River.

In those days Britain was Spain's mortal and historical enemy, and by doing this Spain supported the Americans in their revolution against Britain.

A total of 2,363 men, women, and children from the Canary Islands had been sent to colonise Louisiana by the end of 1783. Living conditions were difficult in a flat, wet, undeveloped land and vastly different from their volcanic island homeland in the sun.

It is easy to understand the fascination of many Americans with these small volcanic islands just off the coast of Africa. More than two hundred years have passed since the arrival of the Canary Islanders in Louisiana. Spanish surnames are plentiful in Louisiana as well as in other states, and their descendants still treasure the unique heritage of their brave ancestors from the Canary Islands.

The Baby Sellers

Living in present-day Spain and the Canary Islands, it is often hard to remember that Spain has only relatively recently emerged as a successful and fully-fledged democracy after years of fear and repression under the hated Franco regime.

As the last remaining statue, erected by Franco during his dictatorship, was recently removed from Barcelona, most Spaniards look to a time when a thick line can finally be drawn under this black period of the country's history.

It is credit to the strength of personality and character of its people that Spain has achieved so much since the dictator's death, and although not always a popular concept with the British, it must be said that membership of the European Union has also been instrumental in the country's transformation from fascist dictatorship to a highly successful democracy.

Anyone following the TV programme, Eastenders, will no doubt be aware of the much publicised and over hyped 'outcry' to the soap's desperate storyline about a stolen baby over the Christmas and New Year period.

Christmas just wouldn't be Christmas without a grim Eastenders' story line to go with the Christmas pudding would it? Do we care anyway? Sadly, there are echoes of the drama currently happening in Tenerife, as well as elsewhere in Spain.

In Santa Cruz, police recently arrested one man and five women, who were offering €10,000 to pregnant, homeless women in exchange for their babies. Police had been watching the suspects for some time after hearing about a person in charge of finding homeless pregnant women who were prepared to give up their babies for cash. Fortunately, the gang have now been detained and charged with crimes against family relationships, as well as attempting to alter the paternity of a child.

Sadly, this tragic story is not new to Spain. Currently there are demands to open a national investigation into allegations that babies were taken away from their mothers at birth and sold to other families for many years, under a law approved by Franco's dictatorship.

It is thought that as many as 300,000 children were stolen in this way during Franco's 1939-75 dictatorship and continued until the late 1980s. This ongoing human tragedy was the result of a 1940 decree that the Spanish state was allowed to take children into custody if their "moral welfare" was at risk.

This left the way open for the dictatorship to take children of jailed left-wing opponents from their families, with state approval and often with the blessing of the Roman Catholic Church, in an attempt to purify Spain of Marxist influence.

Historians now reveal that many of these stolen children were given to religious orders and eventually became monks and nuns, whilst others were adopted illegally by families and given changed identities. Currently, legal cases are continuing against doctors and nurses who participated in the policy and also continued with this illegal business by providing babies for childless couples.

One heartbreaking side of the story, which in so many ways follows the much-criticised Eastenders' storyline, was that new mothers were told that their babies had died within hours of birth. The hospitals told mothers that they had taken care of their burials when in fact the babies had been given to another family.

Fortunately, the story is now fully in the open and an association acting for the victims is now pressing for a full national enquiry into the allegations. Maybe the Eastenders' storyline isn't so far fetched after all?

Lighthouses and Lime Kilns

There are many lighthouses in the Canary Islands, and locals and many visitors will know that there is a particularly fine one at Maspalomas in Gran Canaria. The lighthouse, or Faro in Spanish, helps sailors to navigate their ships and is an integral part of sea-life. Usually, they are cylindrical towers with a light on top, and emit a fixed sequence of beams that is unique to a particular lighthouse.

Built in 1980, the Maspalomas lighthouse is still operational and, for those who like full details, provides 3 white flashes every 13 seconds. Before lighthouses were invented, sailors were warned of hazards by the lighting of fires along the coastline.

Since visiting these islands for the first time many years ago, I am often amazed to discover the strategic and important place that these small islands and its people have in history. Indeed, these islands pack a far greater punch than their size would lead most to believe. The development of the lighthouse is just one of these intrigues. Let us now visit Plymouth in Devon, and stand on Plymouth Hoe, looking out to sea into the impressive expanse of Plymouth Sound...

About 14 miles from the coast stands the Eddystone Lighthouse, which is the fourth lighthouse to be built on the treacherous Eddystone Rocks. Earlier attempts had either caught fire or were washed away, with the exception of one. This was the lighthouse called Smeaton's Tower, which now stands proudly on Plymouth Hoe and was once used to guard against those treacherous rocks.

In 1756, an engineer called John Smeaton was asked by the Royal Society to design the third Eddystone Lighthouse. His inspiration was to be an oak tree - a tall, natural object that could withstand gales without breaking. He used 1,493 blocks of stone, rather like the rings of a tree, dove-tail jointed together with marble dowels and oak pins. Now this is the clever part, Smeaton also pioneered the use of hydraulic lime, a form of concrete that would set under water. This lime came from Arinaga, in Gran Canaria.

Since ancient times, the small coastal town of Arinaga, operated a small cottage industry for the extraction and burning of lime. Quicklime from the Arinaga furnaces was sold throughout the islands and beyond its shores, which led to increased prosperity and economic expansion. It was this quicklime from Arinaga that made the building of Smeaton's Tower possible.

In the early twentieth century, the first cement plant in Arguineguin opened and demanded a lot of hydraulic lime, as well as being needed for agriculture, buildings, ports and roads. Most of the lime produced in Gran Canaria came from Arinaga, where dozens of workers worked in this industry.

The industry is now long gone, but some of the old furnaces have been carefully restored and preserved and can still be seen at the end of the beach in Arinaga, as a memento of its proud contribution to the building industry on the island and beyond.

It is inspiring to think that a combination of Smeaton's inspired design and highly advanced engineering skills still required the contribution of Canary Islanders over 2000 miles away! Smeaton's Tower protected shipping in Plymouth Sound for 120 years and when it was finally replaced in 1882, and was dismantled stone by stone and rebuilt on Plymouth Hoe. It still stands as a permanent reminder of the very clever engineer who created it, with just a little help from the lime workers of Arinaga!

The Ship that Died

I am not a great lover of things nautical; after all, I tend to get seasick when having a bath if the water is too deep.

However, the recent announcement of a new ferry service from Las Palmas in Gran Canaria to Huelva in Peninsular Spain, with a journey time of just over one day, as compared to nearly three days on the alternative service, set me thinking about a once-beautiful ship now lying off a beach on our neighbouring island of Fuerteventura.

This is the story of SS America, a luxury liner that was launched the day before Hitler invaded Poland and brought the world to war in 1939. It was not an auspicious start for a cruise liner that had to be immediately converted into a troop carrier that would not carry the planned 1200 passengers on a luxury cruise, but was destined to become a troop-carrying vessel that would carry up to 8000 troops to war.

The ship was renamed, West Point, and she carried troops around the world. Later, she was confined to the North Atlantic route where her speed and manoeuvrability were ideal to outwit German U boats, gale force winds and the treacherous sea. Troops were carried from the USA to Europe and wounded soldiers, as well as prisoners of war, shipped back to America.

After wartime duties, the SS America resumed life as a cruise ship and was seen as one of the most beautiful of the American fleet. After 24 years of service, the ship's career came to an abrupt end due to labour disputes and the growing popularity of air travel.

The SS America was sold to a Greek shipping company, renamed Australis, and began a new life transporting British passengers who were emigrating to a new life in Australia, as part of a campaign to increase its population.

Later, the assisted passage scheme was gradually phased out and long haul flights made air travel more attractive than a long voyage at sea, and in 1977 the Australis made her last voyage to Australia. There were attempts to reinstate the ship for cruises once again. The SS America was given her original name and intended to resume life as a floating casino.

The first voyage in 1978 was a disaster and angry passengers forced the ship to return to port. The shipping company was sued for $2.5 million and the SS America was held as a surety against debt; the ship's fate was sealed, and the SS America was to be auctioned.

The vessel was then repurchased by her previous Greek owners and was intended to be used as a Mediterranean cruise ship. Italis, as she was renamed, never put to sea. She was sold again in 1980 and renamed Noga, and this time destined to be a floating hotel in Beirut.

This plan did not materialise and so this once proud ship was due to be returned to the USA to become a prison ship, but that fell through too. She was sold again and renamed Alferdoss, which means 'Paradise' in Arabic. Sadly, it was nothing like paradise and for ten years the ship rotted until damage to her bilge pipe meant that she had to be beached to prevent sinking.

Finally, a consortium bought her and gave her yet another new name, the America Star. A star she was no longer and, as she was being towed to Thailand to be converted into a floating hotel, the towrope broke in stormy weather off Fuerteventura.

She broke into two pieces and what little remains has been slowly disappearing into the sea, leaving part of the bow remaining above the water. This once proud vessel is waiting to be finally claimed by the sea.

Camels and Cauliflowers

I remember once being told by a zookeeper that there is nothing tastier for a camel to eat than a nice fresh cauliflower. I doubt that many of these grow in the desert, and remember thinking at the time that it was a tall story intended to satisfy the curiosity of child's endless questioning. I suspect camels will eat anything that they can get their teeth into.

These majestic yet strange creatures look almost out of place in today's world, yet still continue their role as a beast of burden in many countries, because of their ability to travel great distances across hot, dry deserts with little food or water. They are perfectly designed to walk easily on soft sand where vehicles could not travel, and to carry people and heavy loads to places that have no roads.

I was looking at some old photographs of life in the Canary Islands a few days ago. I felt a certain déjà vu as I was looking at the old sepia coloured prints, because they reminded me of some old family photographs that I had seen in my mother's photograph album many years ago.

These were of my grandfather and great-grandfather ploughing a field in rural Lincolnshire, with the help of some magnificent looking horses. The photographs of men and animals working the land in the Canary Islands looked remarkably similar, except instead of horses they were using camels.

Until relatively recent times, it was camels and not horses that were used as the beast of burden on these islands. The first camels were brought to the Canary Islands from Africa in the late fourteenth century, and these creatures were essential for the European colonisation of the islands.

Being so close to Africa, the camels adapted perfectly to the hot and dry conditions in the Canary Islands, and particularly in the south of Gran Canaria and Tenerife, as well as Lanzarote and Fuerteventura. As well as having an important role to play in agriculture, they were perfect for carrying people and goods.

The Canarian Camel, or Camello Canario, is a dromedary, which as I recall from my early school days, has one hump and can be remembered because of the shape of letter 'D' in dromedary. Its cousin, the Bactrian camel has two humps, as in the shape of the letter 'B'.

There are around 1200 camels still on the islands and the indigenous population of the dromedary are the only breed to be recognised as a breed in its own right in Europe and has been recently included in the official Spanish records of livestock breeds.

Nowadays, of course, the Canarian camel is mostly used in the tourist industry as a means of transport on excursions in the islands' national parks and nature reserves, as well as Maspalomas beach.

The islands' camels are also very busy on the night of the Three Kings in January when they are paraded through the streets of many towns on the islands.

As for camels and cauliflowers, I have since found out from a very knowledgeable camel keeper that desert camels are usually fed dates, grass, wheat and oats. In zoos, camels are fed hay and grain, which is about 3.5 kilograms of food everyday. However, if food is very scarce, a camel will eat anything and even its owner's tent!

Admiral Nelson and the Canary Islands

You may remember Horatio Nelson from school history lessons as the jolly little man with the big hat and equally inflated ego; his costume goes down a treat at fancy dress parties.

In pictures, Nelson is instantly recognisable as the semi-blinded, one-armed naval officer who destroyed the French and Spanish fleets; he also had a fascinating ménage à trois with the rather interesting Lady Hamilton. So what is the real story of the man whose statue dominates London's Trafalgar Square, and how does it link with the Canary Islands?

I am often surprised to discover that these lumps of volcanic rock, known as the Canary Islands, punch well above their weight when it comes to links with famous and interesting people, as well as key moments in history; the links with Admiral Nelson are yet another example.

According to the history books, Nelson lost his right eye capturing Corsica and his right arm whilst attacking the Canary Islands. He captured six and destroyed seven of Napoleon's ships at the Battle of the Nile, trapped Napoleon in Egypt, assaulted Copenhagen and dealt with Napoleon's combined French and Spanish fleets off the coast of Spain.

This defeat of the French navy stopped Napoleon's power at sea, and with it, his dreams of world domination. Nelson is, of course, best remembered for winning one of the greatest naval battles in history, the Battle of Trafalgar, on 21 October 1805.

The Battle of Santa Cruz de Tenerife was launched by Nelson on 22 July 1797, and was heavily defeated. British soldiers who succeeded in reaching the beach were riddled with bullets fired by the citizens of Santa Cruz; indeed, these citizens were so closely involved in repelling the attack that many were given honours and medals.

Three days later, the remains of the British landing party withdrew under a truce, which allowed the remaining British forces to return to their ships with full military honours. Part of the truce included an undertaking not to burn the town, or make any further attacks on Tenerife or the Canary Islands. The British fleet had received a painful defeat and would never again attempt to capture Santa Cruz, yet Nelson was given a hero's welcome back in England.

The Spanish suffered 30 dead and 40 injured, whilst the British lost 250 and 128 men were wounded. Nelson had lost many men and ships and so the journey back to England was going to be a problem. In a generous act of chivalry, General Gutiérrez let Nelson borrow two Spanish ships to help the British to get home, as well as allowing the British to leave with their arms and war honours.

These acts of chivalry led to a friendly exchange of letters between Nelson and Gutiérrez. However, Nelson would later comment that Tenerife had been the most horrible hell he had ever endured. Nelson's letter, offering a tasty cheese as a token of gratitude, is on display at the Spanish Army Museum in Toledo.

Nelson himself had been wounded in the arm, which resulted in partial amputation. Nelson's operation was quick and the limb was thrown overboard, despite the admiral's wish to keep it, presumably as a macabre souvenir. Or was it?

One of the parts of this story that intrigues me is that during the assault against Tenerife are claims that Nelson's arm was kept as a souvenir and later stored behind the altar in Las Palmas Cathedral in Gran Canaria.

Whether there is any truth in this story seems unlikely because it would have been against Roman Catholic rules, as only the relics of saints are kept under altars. Nelson may have been a great man, but a saint he was not. Maybe his arm was an exception to the rule?

Interestingly, Canarians also regard Nelson as a great man, and the date of Nelson's defeat, 25 July, is still a public holiday in Santa Cruz de Tenerife where he is described as, "The most gallant enemy we ever had."

Although some sections of my old school history book are questionable, Nelson was certainly an outstanding naval commander. However, he did say, "Kiss me, Hardy," and Captain Thomas Hardy did kiss him, twice.

Sadly though, Nelson never wore an eye patch, so do remember this minor detail the next time you hire a costume for a fancy dress party.

Slavery in the Canary Islands

The horrors of slavery remain a blot upon the human conscience and collective human history. However, even in modern times, despite being outlawed many years ago, slavery still continues in various forms, such as prostitution and trafficking, around the world, including in many 'civilised' European cities. The Canary Islands have a story to tell about this perfect example of "man's inhumanity to man".

The Spanish occupation of the Canary Islands coincided with the massive deportation of the native Guanches from these islands, many of whom were sent as slaves to Spain and other European countries. The Guanches who remained on the islands were forced to work on the estates and businesses run by their new masters.

The ownership of the Canary Islands had been the subject of a long running dispute between Portugal and the Kingdom of Castille for many years. This period of instability and effective rule resulted in periodic raids on the islands to acquire slaves.

The Catholic Church developed an early form of an anti-slavery policy in the 15th century that, to its credit, attempted to rescue many Canary Islanders from the horrors of the Atlantic Slave Trade.

A papal decree, known as Sicut Dudum, was issued in 1435 by Pope Eugene IV, and sent to the Bishop of Lanzarote, which was intended to prohibit Portuguese traders from capturing and incarcerating slaves from the Canary Islands, and shipping them across the Atlantic.

Sadly, this decree only applied to those who had recently converted to Christianity or were, more likely, tricked into baptism, and threatened much dreaded excommunication to those who failed to return the newly processed Christians to the Canary Islands. This decree appears, at first light, to be an enlightened step during those turbulent times to protect Canary Islanders from the evils of this horrendous trade in human lives.

However, although African converts to Christianity were now protected by the papal decree, the same did not apply to Muslims, Jews, heathens or atheists who were still considered to be 'fair game' by the Vatican.

Whatever the truth behind Pope Eugene's original intentions, his successor, Pope Nicholas V, as part of the fight against Islam in 1452, gave the Portuguese king the right to enslave people who were not Christian. Indeed, this agreement was used by the Portuguese to enslave Africans for many years to come.

Needless to say, there have been many attempts over the years by Christian academics to credit the Vatican as taking the first steps towards the banning of slavery and crediting Pope Eugene 1V, in particular, with enlightened views about freedom and morality, which many present day historians and academics say he simply does not deserve.

Sadly, the truth in the Canary Islands seems to be that you either converted in a manner dictated by Pope Eugene IV or risked being rounded up by the Portuguese and sold into slavery - not really much of a choice, was it?

The religious concept of free will appears to have been forgotten too, and due to be repeated many times in the future, with Jewish and Muslim converts joining the ranks of Christianity to avoid the violent machine of the Spanish Inquisition.

Still, as we all know, the rewriting of history is a popular pastime, as well as a strategy much loved by some politicians, historians and newspapers. Maybe some things will never change.

Wear White and Throw Talcum Powder!

I am not a violent man, and I detest violence of all kind. However, I do make an exception for just one day each year in the Canary Islands - Dia de Los Indianos (Day of the Indians).

As many Canary Islander residents and visitors already know, Carnival is celebrated with a passion in every major town in each of the seven main Canary Islands, with the main celebrations taking place in the capital cities of the islands. These celebrations take place between January and April each year with the actual dates changing according to when Easter is celebrated; this is most annoying for holidaymakers, but take that issue up with the Vatican!

The forty days before Easter, known as Lent, have always been marked by the Catholic practice of giving up meat. So the fiesta of Carnival that takes place just before Lent begins on Shrove Tuesday or Mardi Gras. Carnival means 'goodbye to flesh' in Latin and became a time for a wild party, and yes, I do mean wild!

There are references to Carnival in island government records as far back as February 1556, but the fiesta has grown from strong influences from South America and the Caribbean, as many Canarians left the islands after the Spanish Conquest seeking work or their fortunes in the newly discovered lands of the Americas.

Some islanders were forced to leave their homes in the Canary Islands by the Spanish government, as it wanted more people to settle in the Spanish colonies in the Americas. Later, many Canary Islanders returned home, having made their fortune, dressed in Cuban-style white panama hats, and carrying large suitcases full of money. These newly wealthy emigrants were so full of their own self-importance, bragging about their riches, that they became the target of Carnival jokes.

On the small Canary island of La Palma they hold a unique fiesta called Fiesta de Los Indianos - The Festival of the Indians - and now often called the White Party. On the Monday before Shrove Tuesday or Mardi Gras, the city of Santa Cruz de La Palma celebrates Los Indianos Fiesta.

This is a celebration of those who emigrated from the island many years ago, particularly for islands in the Caribbean and South America and then returned having made their fortune. The fiesta is a representation of people wearing white suits and costumes of an earlier colonial period; some portray the wealthy and some are their servants. The parade takes place through the streets of the capital to the sound of Latin American music.

The main event of the day is the Batalla de Polvos de Talco when bags of talcum powder are thrown at anyone standing nearby. So, by the end of the battle, most people have white hair and faces, as well as white clothes.

The traditions of this important part of La Palma's Carnival have been 'borrowed' over the years and now play a full part in the Carnival activities of the other Canary Islands. On Carnival Monday, the streets of Santa Cruz de La Palma, as well as Las Palmas de Gran Canaria, will fill with thousands of white-clad revellers and huge clouds of talcum powder in this eccentric celebration.

Now, that is what I call a real fight and, hopefully, no one gets hurt! Maybe I should suggest this to the United Nations as a way of settling international disputes.

Living on a Volcano

Shortly after moving to the Costa Blanca, we discovered that an earthquake had destroyed a small town close to the urbanisation where we had made our home in the nineteenth century.

Nowadays, we live on a volcanic island in an archipelago where there are still several active volcanoes.

One of the very first pieces of advice that we received when we arrived in the Costa Blanca, and one that we quickly learned to be particularly valuable, was "Never believe what you hear from bar gossip; always find out the facts for yourselves."

Bar chat is easy and, like Chinese Whispers, often varies significantly from the truth, and particularly if it is bad or disturbing news.

However, many expats, desperate for information and advice in their own language, often readily fall for misleading information.

The current topic in many of the Brit bars in the Canary Islands is the issue of seismic shocks currently underway in one of our neighbouring islands, El Hierro.

This island paradise is quickly becoming the source of overreaction and potentially dangerous gossip causing concern. So what exactly are the issues?

Over the last few weeks, seismic shocks on El Hierro, which the experts call 'swarms' have been mostly of low magnitude since they started in early July, and most of the seismic activity has been limited to about 9 to 16 kilometres below the surface.

The question on everyone's mind is, "Is El Hierro heading for an eruption and, if not, what is going on beneath the surface?"

We need to remember that the Canary Islands are volcanic in origin and a wide variety of lava has erupted from Canary Island volcanoes over the years.

Without the volcanic eruptions in the past there would be no Canary Islands. Experts tell us that they are similar to the volcanoes found in Hawaii, and that they share many similarities in that they can grow very large and that the style of eruption and lava flow are similar.

Should we be surprised by this seismic activity at El Hierro? The answer seems to be: No.

Although the islands' volcanoes are nowhere near as productive as Hawaii or indeed Iceland, the Canary hotspot is one of the more vigorous on the planet.

Does this seismic activity automatically lead to an eruption? Not necessarily, and this activity might not even lead to an eruption.

However, now that we have many of these volcanic systems so closely monitored, we notice this subtle activity as it happens, rather than waiting until we can feel the seismic activity on the surface, which usually means that an eruption is highly likely.

In other words, there are plenty of warning systems and the monitoring of seismic activity is constantly taking place.

These incidents should remind us that El Hierro is an active volcano and that these signals are a warning of an eruption sometime in the future.

It is always a good idea to be prepared, especially when living on a volcanic island. Over 10,000 people live on El Hierro, and emergency planning will tell residents what to do and where to go if El Hierro does decide to erupt.

However, most eruptions produce lava flows and ash that are not likely to be a major threat to the island's residents unless they are caught unaware, which is highly unlikely.

People on Hawaii have been living with a constantly erupting volcano for over 30 years, Mount Etna in Sicily performs a regular firework display, as do the volcanoes in Iceland; so any activity on El Hierro should be impressive to watch, but not a catastrophe for the residents of the island, nor indeed for the rest of the Canary Islands. So back to your gin and tonics and the sun beds; you now have the facts and not just the bar gossip.

Live and Let Live

One of the many things that I love about our island in the sun is the 'live and let live' attitude of most of its people.

No, I don't mean the thousands of tourists, but the true Canarian people, those who were born here and have stayed in this little corner of Paradise.

As long as it is broadly legal and does not interfere with anyone else, in the main, anything goes. For many of its present day expat population, with its heady mix of faith, culture, colour and sexuality, it takes time to get used to not being judged.

Maybe this stems from the time, it is said, when Spain's General Franco, intolerant of gay men in the military, would ship them off to Gran Canaria, which became a kind of penal colony for homosexuals.

Whether there is real historical substance to this claim or whether it is an urban myth, I do not know for sure, but it sounds reasonable enough to me, although I am quite sure that the Yumbo Centre wasn't there then!

For me, one of the real unsung heroes of the Second World War was the code-breaker, Alan Turing.

23 June 2012 saw the centenary of his birth and it was thanks to this mathematical genius that the war against Nazi Germany ended two years earlier than it otherwise would have done.

48

He managed to intercept and crack ingenious coded messages that gave detailed information to the Allies about the activities of German U-boats.

However, in the eyes of many, there was only one problem with Alan Turing - he was gay.

Alan's reward for his pivotal role in cracking intercepted messages was quickly forgotten when, in 1952, he was prosecuted for 'indecency' after admitting a sexual relationship with a man.

As an 'alternative' to imprisonment, this unsung war hero was given 'chemical castration' - a newly devised treatment for such 'disorders' at the time.

In 1954, at the age of 41, he killed himself by eating a poisoned apple, which was apparently inspired by the story of Snow White.

Needless to say, as with much of history, this version of events is currently being challenged and massaged for the financial gains for another film, documentary or book.

However, I rather like the original version of the tragedy, agreed by the coroner at the time; it is just so dramatic!

Or was this the end of Alan Turing? This amazing man is also credited with creating the beginnings of computer technology and artificial intelligence, which led to the development of one of the first recognisable modern computers.

Alan Turing's brilliance and personal life came to the attention of present day computer programmer, Dr. John Graham-Cumming, who began a petition asking for a posthumous apology from the government.

Many thousands of people signed it and a previous UK Prime Minister, Gordon Brown, finally apologised for how Alan Turing was treated in the 1950s.

Whether it was through political motivation or genuine compassion for this brilliant man, and I like to think it is the latter, he said that "on behalf of the British government, and all those who live freely thanks to Alan's work, I am very proud to say: we're sorry, you deserved so much better."

My thoughts also go out to the many thousands of gay men and woman who have been persecuted over the years - just for being themselves.

All this serious stuff brings me back home to Gran Canaria. Spain's General Franco certainly had his faults, but I cannot help thinking that being shipped off to a life in the sun in the penal colony of Gran Canaria, just for being gay, was a far preferable alternative to 'chemical castration'!

Mystery, Awe and Wonder

The
Canary
Islander

Do you suffer from Paraskavedekatriaphobia?

We have a lot to thank the Greeks for and, no, I am not being sarcastic about the level of Greek debt. I am referring to the ability of the Greek language to make something quite ordinary sound rather special, and particularly, if there is a phobia attached to it for good measure.

So, in this rather splendid word, Paraskevi (or Paraskeve) is Friday in Greek, Dekatria is thirteen, and phobia is a word that we all know. Paraskavedekatriaphobia is the fear of Friday 13th.

So what is it about Friday 13th? This day has been associated with market crashes and other disasters for many centuries.

It is also believed that Jesus was crucified on a Friday and, in Britain, Friday the 13th was execution day and later Hangman's day, or the 'Witches Sabbath'.

Hindus believed that it was unlucky for thirteen people to gather in one place and perhaps the best known symbolism of this is the biblical 'Last Supper'; if thirteen people dine together, one will die.

However, it is not always Friday that is the day of bad luck. In Spain, and other Spanish speaking countries, the saying "Martes trece, ni te cases, ni te embarques, ni de tu casa te apartes" has particular relevance.

When translated it means, "On Tuesday the 13th don't marry or board a ship, or even leave your house".

In Spain and Greece, Tuesday 13th is thought to be an unlucky day and in Italy it is Friday 17th that is considered unlucky.

While the origins of these unlucky days are debatable, the impact of them can be disturbing and cause considerable stress to may people around the world.

Research from the USA alone considers that 21 million people have a genuine fear of this unlucky day.

What about the Chinese? They have to be careful to avoid occurrences or reminders of the number 4 during festive holidays, or when a family member is sick. Similarly, 14, 24, 34 etc are also to be avoided due to the presence of the digit 4 in these numbers. In China, these floor numbers are often avoided in hotels, offices and apartments.

Table numbers 4, 14, 24 etc are also missed out in wedding receptions or other social gatherings. In Hong Kong, some apartments have missed out all the floors from 40 to 49.

Immediately above the 39th floor is the 50th, leading many who are not aware of tetraphobia to believe that some floors are missing.

In cities where East Asian and Western cultures blend, such as Hong Kong and Singapore, it is possible in some buildings that both 13 and 14 are skipped as floor numbers along with all the other 4's and so it goes on.

Indeed, the Finnish telecommunications firm, Nokia, also observes this superstition and try to avoid releasing any phone models that begin with the number 4, except in some rare cases, "as a gesture to Asian customers."

Am I superstitious? Certainly not. However, I would rather not walk under a ladder, I am not sure about black cats, and I do think a shamrock is a rather good thing to have...

Well, it is always better to be safe than sorry, isn't it? I had better come clean about one thing though - I was born on Friday 13th, so I am not paraskavedekatriaphobic.

Imaginary noises?

I wonder if any readers have been plagued with a strange noise that they cannot find or understand? I had such an experience last week that troubled me greatly. Try as I may, I could not trace the origin of the squeaking noise in my study.

At first, I thought it was a mobile phone or a gadget that needed recharging. Maybe it was a clock that needed oiling, or maybe it was a mouse? I called in our local expert on such matters, Mac our cat.

He listened intently, but then paid no further attention and wandered off. Clearly it was a sound that was not coming from vermin, and he was not interested. I had to investigate further myself.

The problem reminded me of another incident some time ago. A retired couple were deeply concerned about their coffee table that had suddenly developed a ticking sound.

Brenda thought that she was hearing things. Every time she entered part of the living room, she heard the strange sound, and she was certain that it was not a clock or an electrical device.

Maybe it was from next door? The ticking went on all day and all night – only it was much louder at night. Sometimes when she came into the room at night it sounded more of a scratching – was it mice or maybe rats? Colin, her husband, also heard the strange noise.

Eventually, the couple, through a process of elimination, traced the sound to a coffee table in their living room. It was a rather lovely wood coffee table, purchased over two years ago from a furniture shop in Spain, and was part of a traditional dining suite.

It was made of pine, but stained a darker colour in true Spanish style. The table was silent for the first six months, but had since found a voice of its own.

Since the scratching/ticking/clicking noise started, friends were invited in to listen and they too confirmed that the strange noises were coming from the table, and that the sound appeared to be coming from one leg in particular.

Many solutions were offered. Maybe the leg could be cut off? What about fumigation? How about painting it with a drop of alcohol? All the ideas were rejected because, it appears, that Brenda and Colin had become rather fond of the creature within – and they wanted to see what would happen next.

Brenda had also recently spotted a small amount of dust around the table leg and was anxious that the creature did not infest other furniture in the house.

Brenda was convinced that it was not just woodworm, and that the eggs or larvae of the creature were already within the wood when the table was made.

Later, the couple happened to meet an entomologist on holiday and discussed the problem with him.

He visited the couple's home, and identified 'the bug' as 'Spondylis Buprestoides' and explained about the creature's life cycle.

Apparently, the creature starts off life as one of many eggs hidden behind the bark of a pine tree. The incubation period is between one and five years, but may be as long as ten years – dependent upon climatic conditions.

Presumably, once it has been made into furniture and moved into a warm, sunny room in Spain, this hastens the process.

The creature then eats its way out of its woody incubator, goes through three stages as a chrysalis and then finally emerges as a beetle. The beetle is then ready to do what all beetles do to ensure continuation of the species.

I cannot help but to feel some admiration for this creature and for its determination to survive. Brenda and Colin's furniture had been through a manufacturing process of dipping and staining before they purchased it, yet these creatures survived even these toxic processes.

So, what about the noise in my study? Sadly, it was nothing quite as exciting or as exotic as Spondylis Buprestoides, but a UPS unit (used to provide a buffer of power to my computer during our regular power cuts), which had reached the end of its useful life and was telling me that it needed to be replaced.

"The Stars Smile Down on You"

Those who have easy access to BBC television may have seen the recent series, 'The Wonders of the Solar System', hosted by the equally wondrous Professor Brian Cox, which has inspired me to take much more notice of the night sky.

After all, the Canary Islands are very well placed for stargazing. During these programmes, I also wished that such a passionate and enthusiastic teacher as Brian Cox had taught me during those interminably boring physics lessons when I was a pupil at school.

Apart from one memorable experience, my studies were a very boring diet of what seemed like useless information and regurgitated facts that had no relevance to the world that I lived in. Why were we not told more about the wonders of the universe and information that related to our very being?

No, the highlight of my career in physics was a pinhole camera that I made after one lesson about light, when I was suddenly and surprisingly inspired. This happened to be the beginning of my interest in photography and so possibly those boring physics lessons were not completely wasted on me after all.

My pinhole camera experiment was a revelation in more ways than one, because in the process of testing the quality of focus, a friend and I decided to photograph the rear of a teacher's car in the staff car park thinking that we could use the vehicle's number plate as a test card.

It was after we had spotted that the parked car was swaying gently from side to side that we realised that we had discovered a passionate relationship between a member of staff and the pretty French language exchange student in the back of the Morris Minor that we were photographing.

Needless to say, for two curious eleven-year-olds, the whole experience was an interesting revelation into the ways of the world and made for an interesting physics lesson after all.

Returning to the television programme and the wonders of the Solar System where our own small planet Earth was both celebrated, as well as placed into the much wider context of the solar system and beyond.

From this programme, I began to understand one of the sayings about the Canary Islands, possibly used far too much by travel agencies, as a place where "The stars smile down on you". Physics now, at last, began to make some sense.

Sky watching is at its best in the Canary Islands where the night skies are mostly crystal clear thanks to the efforts of successive islands' Governments over the years to reduce light pollution.

The location of the Canary Islands also means that we can see all the constellations of the northern hemisphere throughout the year and mostly without the help of a telescope.

As our eyes become accustomed to the night sky, we can get a flavour of the vastness of the universe and suddenly thousands of stars seem to appear and form a glittering blanket; if we are really fortunate we can sometimes see shooting stars as well.

A high position away from the main centre of population gives the best view or, in my case, a quick stroll to the seashore is usually good enough for a spectacular viewing.

It is wonderful how new information and earlier gained knowledge sometimes just falls into place when inspired or we are somehow reminded at a much later time.

For me, stargazing has been a revelation, although I do still wonder how two grown adults managed to do anything of significance in such a small car! Mind you, they may just have been conjugating verbs!

Environmental

The
Canary
Islander

Energy Island

We hear a lot about global warming, renewable energy and climate change nowadays. The need seems to be clear enough but, as yet, only around 12.9% of the energy supply required by the world comes from renewable sources.

Of that, about half comes from the burning of wood for heat and cooking in developing countries, which causes other problems. In addition, these sources are not always renewable, because they depend upon new trees being planted, which is often overlooked.

The fastest growing technology is solar electric power, yet this continues to be among the most expensive option and will continue to be so for several more years.

The good news is that a recent report on climate change says that renewable technologies could provide 80 per cent of the world's energy needs in the next thirty years or so.

However, there is a solution closer to hand than we may think, and that solution is just a few hops across the water to one of our beautiful islands - El Hierro, once known as 'Fire Island'.

El Hierro gained its original name of 'Fire Island' from its origins of volcanic eruptions many years ago, and although volcanic activity has decreased, the natural Earth forces of water and wind remain.

These power sources are now due to be harnessed so that by 2012, this small island in the Atlantic will be the first to be able to generate all of its electricity needs from sources that are renewable.

There is plenty of wind on El Hierro and visitors will have noticed that the reason that most plants and trees seem to be suffering from osteoporosis is that they have become bent by its force.

There is enough rain to meet the needs of the 10,700 inhabitants of the island, and the five wind turbines in the north east of the island will produce enough electric power to supply all of the island's energy needs, as well as pumping water from a reservoir near the harbour to a bigger reservoir at a higher level within a volcanic crater.

What if there is no wind? Well, in that case, water is released from the higher reservoir through these pipes that will drive hydraulic turbines to create electric energy. Therefore, electricity can be produced by wind or water power. Clever stuff!

This project in El Hierro is the first that does not use electricity produced from traditional methods, and contributes to moving the island towards being totally self-sufficient. When the project is completed in 2012, this renewable energy project will produce three times the island's needs for electricity, including electricity for 60,000 tourists who visit each year.

Also, when there is a surplus of electricity produced, this will be used for three desalination plants to convert seawater into fresh water for irrigation.

In 2012, the oil-fired electricity power station that currently produces electricity for the island will close, reducing carbon emissions and saving on the cost of importing 6000 tonnes of oil each year.

Although this renewable energy project will have cost €65 million, future income from this energy source will eventually repay this investment, cover future maintenance and replacement costs, and still make a profit.

This project alone means that the island will meet 100% of its energy needs by 2015, but El Hierro has launched other sustainability projects too. The island is mainly agricultural, and is a leader in organic farming, as well as in projects that convert sewage into fertiliser and methane.

Even more energy savings are planned after 2012 by replacing all the cars on the island with electric vehicles, and although the investment costs for charging terminals and purchasing the vehicles will need a similar investment to the wind energy project, this would be repaid in ten years, assuming that drivers are charged the same price as for petrol.

Yes, there is always a catch!

Lizards Prefer Islands

One of Bella's favourite pastimes is lizard hunting. Bella is unlike any other dog that we have known, and her terrier nature is certainly one of her very prominent features.

If it moves she will chase it, whereas Barney, our self-willed corgi, would just look at something thrown for him to fetch, stare back at us with a "fetch it yourself" look and wander away for yet another snooze in the sun.

On our walks, Bella loves to run on the sunny sandy or rocky wasteland areas where she knows that she will find many an unsuspecting lizard peacefully sunbathing. Fortunately, they are all far too quick for her; they hear us coming and scurry away before Bella can catch them.

These creatures fascinate me, and when I am walking on my own without Bella, I watch them carefully. I have the same feeling about lizards as I do tortoises, crocodiles, elephants and camels.

They represent an age long gone, and seem almost stranded in the modern day world.

I am told that lizards in the Canary Islands are harmless and do not attack people. They often live in the gaps between rocks, as well as in walls, and I know of tourists in some areas who have fed them when they have appeared in their holiday accommodation.

Apparently, they like to eat crumbs, cactus flowers, grapes, biscuits and fresh fruit, as well as fresh hibiscus flowers. It is the females who are the friendliest of the species and may even jump on your hand for a while, whilst the males are very territorial.

Tourists often spot them basking in the sun on a really hot day on their stomachs and with their feet off the ground. They are certainly fascinating creatures to watch.

Several species of lizard exist uniquely in the Canary Islands, including the Canary Gecko, which is found nowhere else on earth, and thrives on the smaller islands. Indeed, it seems that lizards prefer islands.

Scientific research has shown that this is because limited areas and isolation on islands reduces the number of likely predators and competition pressures.

As a result, island lizards are able to reach exceptionally high population densities. I am not a lizard expert, but I am aware of a fascinating story about lizards that relates to one of the smaller Canary Islands, the island of La Palma and the La Palma Giant Lizard.

The La Palma Giant Lizard disappeared about 500 years ago. It was one of countless species that was thought to be extinct.

It was believed to have gone into decline with the arrival of humans on its native home in the Canary Islands. However, in 2007 one was discovered alive and well on the island.

Little is known about these lizards, but the one that was found measured about 30 centimetres long - a size that Bella would not approve of.

Researchers hope to revisit the island over time in an attempt to find a breeding population.

Two other species of giant lizards have been rediscovered in the Canary Islands in recent times such as in 1974 and 1999, the El Hierro Giant Lizard and La Gomera Giant Lizard.

As I chase across the rough ground with Bella in the hunt for yet another phantom lizard, I try to tell Bella that she will never catch one, so why bother?

It would be much more fun to chase her ball instead. She ignores me and I suspect that she lives in the hope that one day her opportunity will come.

Daring to dream the impossible

Teachers have a responsibility to ensure that their pupils can read and write, and are numerate. It is a stated aim that they should do well in their SATS and achieve good grades in their GCSEs and beyond.

However, education is much more than this and wise teachers place learning about life, learning to being happy and fulfilled human beings, as well as daring to dream the unthinkable at the very top of their priorities.

By this I mean that creativity, and the ability for clear thinking, as well as original thinking, are all necessary for the process of 'real education' to be successful and for the ultimate survival of the species.

I like to hear stories of people defying the odds, achieving the unachievable and daring to be different. When faced with crises and potential disaster the human race has always had a remarkable capacity for daring to dream the impossible to get out of a tight corner.

Over the years, explorers, wartime leaders, artists, philosophers, musicians and sportsmen and women have all contributed to the feeling that the impossible can not only be dreamt about, but can also be made real. History also teaches us that we are often at our best when faced with a crisis.

Many of us will have witnessed the horror story of drought and famine in Africa unfolding daily on our television screens.

Charitable appeals and harrowing stories are now the nightmare of television news. We want to help, but we often feel helpless against such odds.

However, one man may just have an answer to some of the current problems facing the world. Georges Mougin, often dismissed as a crank, recognised some 40 years ago that 70 per cent of the world's fresh water reserves are locked in the ice caps, yet thousands of people are dying of drought and famine in Africa.

To Georges, the answer is simple - tow giant icebergs thousands of miles from the polar ice caps to Africa or, more precisely, to the Canary Islands.

Georges initially received backing from a Saudi prince; however, experts told him that the project was unworkable and it remained as an idea at the back of his mind for decades.

Computer technology has since demonstrated that his imaginative project to tap into the 'floating water reservoirs' is both achievable and affordable.

3-D computer simulations show that a single tugboat could transport a seven million ton iceberg from Newfoundland to the Canary Islands in less than five months without the iceberg melting.

After a suitable iceberg has been chosen, it is lassoed and an insulating skirt wraps the submerged section of the iceberg. This skirt acts rather like a wetsuit, holding in the melted water and insulating the iceberg.

A tug, assisted by sail and ocean currents, then drags the iceberg, at one knot per hour. 141 days later, the tug and its cargo of ice should arrive in the Canary Islands - considered to be an ideal holding location from where the water can be directed to drought spots in Africa.

Tests indicate that just 38 per cent of the 525ft-deep iceberg would melt during its journey - with plenty of fresh water remaining for drought-ridden areas.

It is calculated that a 30-million ton iceberg could provide 500,000 people with fresh water for a year. Daring to dream the impossible could mean that Georges Mougin, armed with the latest evidence, will be able to fund a trial run next year.

I bet his class teacher would be very proud of him.

Solar Rubbish Bins

A recent visit to the UK, after a break of several years, prompted a number of comments from family and friends about the things that had changed during our time away, along the lines of "Have you noticed many changes?"

Well, the weather was still damp and cold; I was struck by how green and beautiful the countryside looked and there was not a cactus in sight.

I was interested to see how many rather ordinary secondary schools, that I had previously known, now proudly announced that they were 'Academies', although apart from the new signs, I cannot comment whether anything inside these schools had actually improved, or whether the pupils were more academically successful or not.

I did notice that people seemed to be behaving in a more frenetic manner than usual; they looked more troubled than I remember, and most conversations were about "The Recession", "Nick Clegg" or "the demise of the NHS".

The homes of relatives and friends also seemed much colder than I recall, apart from one of my nephews who lit a real log fire to warm us up. Scarily, a few friends and relatives were wearing body-warmers and hats - inside the house!

Maybe after several years of living in the Canary Islands our blood really has thinned, or maybe our families and friends have just turned down their thermostats, because of the horrendous gas and electricity bills.

What really did make an impression upon me were the solar rubbish bins in Bournemouth Gardens. First of all, I was impressed that solar energy was at last being taken seriously by a borough council that is not usually given credit as being particularly forward-looking, but also that any such devices appeared in the UK at all; after all, they do require frequent sunlight.

This very clever machine, affectionately known as the "Big Belly Solar Compactor", looked like many other large metal rubbish bins, but a solar panel provided all the power it needed to compress the rubbish as it became full.

One of the gardeners who was planting seedlings nearby, assured me that the bin now needed emptying every two weeks rather than daily as previously, which I found very hard to believe, given the size of the bin.

Even so, this device should represent a significant saving in manpower over time, assuming that the sun does its bit too. Why do we not have these bins in the place where the sun shines to order, the Canary Islands?

Bearing in mind that the Canary Islands are now home to the largest solar power station in Europe (at Granadilla in Tenerife) and there are many companies dedicated to the development of solar power in the Canary Islands, the lack of solar installations on domestic and commercial properties always surprises me.

Given the heavy increases in electricity bills that all Canary Islanders have had to face in recent years, one would imagine that there would be a huge demand for solar panels, yet I see no evidence of this.

In contrast, our small neighbouring island, El Hierro, is already well known for its recent headline grabbing volcanic eruptions, but less well known for its achievements over a twenty-five year period in making the island fully self sufficient with 100 per cent renewable energy, which is a clear example of what can be achieved with determination, as well as inspiring leadership.

El Hierro, which means "island of fire" – has an abundance of wind and water and, thanks to the combined forces of the two, will shortly be able to provide a supply of clean energy for the islanders.

Until then, most of the electricity needed is from diesel fuel shipped to the island in oil tankers. The new renewable power sources will lead to a reduction of around 18,000 tons of carbon dioxide emissions every year. Given this result for a small island, just think of what could be achieved for larger communities worldwide - solar rubbish bins for all!

Are we bothered?

"What the British can't see won't bother them" was the response from the British Ambassador to Spain when asked about the recent news of the authorisation of an oil company to explore for oil off the Canary Islands.

Although mindful of the creed of most Ambassadors to be "All things to all men" (such is the world of diplomacy), it is understandable that the Ambassador was not in a position to criticise the decision of the Spanish Government.

However, to many Islanders, as well as environmentalists in Spain, his inappropriate and ill-timed comment at the time of the announcement was regarded as unhelpful at best, and insensitive at worst. The islanders are bothered.

It is certainly true that the British like their holidays in the sun, but many are also concerned about environmental dangers facing the world, as well as in an area so rich in marine life as the Canary Islands.

Holidaymakers flock to the islands each year in search of sunshine and beautiful beaches, to enjoy fresh fish and to explore some of the more remote areas in the mountains.

Will they really continue to do so with oil platforms scattered around the area and polluting our ocean? Holidaymakers are bothered.

Most holidaymakers are well aware of the issues surrounding the dangers to the fishing industry and local population should another disaster occur, as in the Gulf of Mexico.

Warnings from Greenpeace too highlight the immense dangers to the environment from all forms of deep-sea exploration. Of course, the irony is that fuel from oil is required to bring holidaymakers to the islands in the first place.

Do we really have to see the dangers before we are aware of them, and become concerned about their impact to ourselves and future generations? Most British holidaymakers are bothered.

The Spanish Government needs more revenue and, in theory, a reduction in oil bills would significantly help the economy in time. The Spanish Government also maintains that their decision will bring much needed revenue and jobs to the islands, as well as Peninsular Spain.

This is indeed tempting, as the islands have one of the largest unemployment statistics in Spain, and the lack of opportunity for its young people is heartbreaking.

However, this claim is disputed by many politicians in the Canary Islands, who comment that most jobs in the new oil industry will go to people from outside the Canary Islands, and its largely unskilled workforce will not be needed and neither, in time, will there be a tourist and fishing industry to sustain them in the traditional manner. Many island workers and young people are bothered.

Ironically, the British government has just given BP the go-ahead to drill a new deep-water well in Scottish waters off the northwest coast of the Shetland Islands.

The issues to be faced in Shetland are very similar to those in the Canary Islands, and environmentalists were outraged with the announcement, quoting the potential risks to the climate and threat of an oil spill.

Is deep-water drilling really worth the risk? Should we not be phasing out our use of oil instead of chasing ever more difficult sources?

These are some of the comments that are currently echoing in both the Canary Islands, as well as the Shetland Islands. Are the Shetland Islanders bothered about the risks to their beautiful and unique islands? Of course they are.

Only last week, investigations began into a large oil spill from a platform in the North Sea that was "allowed to disperse naturally" into the ocean.

The spill of 23 tonnes of crude oil came from the Tern oil platform 100 miles north east of Lerwick, the capital of the Shetland Islands.

The oil company stated that the spill was a result of "a temporary upset in the production process whilst cleaning up a new well", and the spill was stopped quickly and posed no risk to either crew or the platform.

This one incident is a taste of issues that could seriously affect both island archipelagos for generations to come.

I have no answer to the twin dilemmas of the demand for oil balanced with environmental and climatic impact. However, I do know that warnings about the environment and climate change should be taken seriously and that we do need to reduce our dependency upon oil.

Meanwhile, a clear debate about all the issues involved, as well as alternatives to the current proposals are what the inhabitants of both the Shetlands and the Canary Islands require.

Dismissive comments such as those made by the Ambassador about the current proposals are unhelpful. In the words of comedienne, Catherine Tate, yes, we are bothered.

A Prickly Issue

My Great Aunt Gertie sent me a present by post for my seventh birthday. How pleased I was, until I opened it. The package contained a small book, 'The Observer's Book of Cacti'.

Now anyone who really knew me in those days could see that I was besotted with adventure books, books about animals and islands. Indeed, two of my favourite presents were 'The Observer's Book of Dogs' and 'The Observer's Book of Cats', and I really wanted the one about reptiles.

My disappointment was such that I wrote the obligatory thank you letter to Aunt Gertie under sufferance, and as instructed by my mother, and tossed the book ungratefully onto my bookshelf and forgot all about it.

Many years later, I was doing what many would-be expats do before leaving their country of origin, which is the painful decision of what to take and what to leave behind.

My collections of books, records, CDs and cassettes all had to go to the charity shop, and I contented myself with the thought that if there was something that I really wanted in the future, I could buy it again.

In the end, giving all my childhood memories away was just too painful, and I secreted a small collection of books from my childhood in a relative's disused garage.

Recently, I had to return to the UK, and I was drawn to my elderly relative's garage, and discovered the box of books, still languishing where I had left them, but now dusty and covered with cobwebs.

As I sorted through the books, memories came flooding back like old friends. Rupert Annuals, Sooty Annuals, Robinson Crusoe, Swallows and Amazon, The Famous Five and The Secret Seven all brought back happy memories of, what I seem to remember, as endlessly long and hot summer evenings, when I went to bed early and read for hours.

Suddenly, I spotted a book that I did not recall ever opening, 'The Observer's Book of Cacti'.

I sat on the corner of a dusty old bench and flicked through its contents. It was not such a bad book after all. The shiny, printed-paper revealed some good quality photographs, and the text was quite revealing.

I had never realised what very adaptable and hardy plants cactus are. I popped the small book into my rucksack, and was determined to read it in further detail when I arrived home.

It was on the long and tedious flight home to Gran Canaria that I opened the book once again, and suddenly realised an answer to an ongoing problem.

Like so many expats, I miss the greenery, trees and flowers of the UK. I am not a skilful gardener, but I do know what I like.

Occasionally, impulse buying gets the better of me and I am tempted to buy plants that are totally unsuited to the desert conditions in the part of the Canary Islands where I live.

Hydrangeas, rhododendrons, magnolias, azaleas and orchids all suffer the same fate during the hot summer months on this island. Suddenly, it came to me. I knew what I would grow in my garden - cactus, and lots of them!

I have since read The Observer's Book of Cacti in detail, and purchased dozens of flowering cactus for one euro each. These fascinating living gems have beautiful and dramatic flowers, and not the stuck on plastic flowers that adorn the overpriced cactus for sale in UK garden centres.

Several months on, the cactus plants are growing fast and my garden is now full of colour. Finally, I have learned to appreciate cactus and to grow plants to suit where I live, and not to attempt to copy the plants that grew in my previous garden in the UK.

In a way, it is another expat lesson; it is all about recognising and fitting in with where we live, and not trying to make our new surroundings fit around our own limited perspective of life. Thank you, Aunt Gertie.

What a load of old rubbish!

Visitors to smart, upmarket Meloneras and the agreeably tired Playa del Ingles often comment about how well the gardens, roundabouts and public facilities are maintained and that the area is mostly free of litter.

In the main, this is true, and so it should be given the huge amount of tourists that visit the area each year, together with accompanying revenue. Basic cleanliness and tidy, litter free areas are the least that we should be offering our visitors.

Sadly, all is not 'smelling of roses' in some of the outlying areas of the municipality of San Bartolome de Tirajana (often referred to as Maspalomas). Some of the outlying areas and villages are sadly becoming increasingly neglected, refuse collection has been reduced, and rubbish allowed to run riot. One example is in the village of Castillo del Romer

al, a pleasant village, which is mostly ignored by tourists. A central rubbish collection point adjacent to a very pleasant beach and an open air swimming pool has rarely been emptied in recent weeks, and a huge amount of litter including old sofas, cookers, garden furniture and builders' rubble has been allowed to accumulate.

Although the massive skip is compressed and emptied from time to time, it is not frequent enough, and the municipality appears to have given up on removing the larger items and the rubbish that has collected adjacent to it.

The problem is exacerbated by local vagrants who gather, argue and fight for the honour of climbing into the skip and sorting through the rubbish in the forlorn hope of finding something useful to sell and yes, often to eat.

Such desperation is a sign of very difficult times, yet many cannot be bothered to throw unwanted items back into the skip, preferring to strew the area with plastic bags, unwanted fruit, vegetables, left over meat and fish instead.

As a result, vermin, cockroaches and flies are having a wonderful time, and the smell is appalling for local residents and visitors. Even the motor caravans that gather nearby each weekend now give the area a wide berth.

Village locals do not help the situation either. Building rubble, bottles and boxes, broken furniture, unwanted electrical items and broken furniture do not appear miraculously by themselves.

On several occasions I have seen young children and dogs with cut hands, feet and paws from the shards of broken glass strewn nearby.

Our nearest town of Vecindario in the neighbouring municipality of Santa Lucia appears to deal with the issue in a much more practical manner.

Instead of open skips, vulnerable to the wind, vermin and vagrants, neat stainless steel hoppers are installed in the streets, complete with cavernous hoppers hidden beneath, which are regularly emptied by the municipality.

It is impossible to dump large furniture, builders' rubble and garden rubbish in these bins, which instead has to be taken elsewhere, presumably to dump in Castillo del Romeral or another forgotten village in a neighbouring municipality!

Cutbacks, recession, holidays and staffing levels are just some of the excuses that I hear for this current lack of attention to basic refuse management.

For goodness sake, basic hygiene and security are the hallmarks of any civilised society, and it does not require a huge amount of funding to achieve a minimum standard. Let's make a start by cleaning up our own mess.

Places to Visit

The Canary Islander

Head for the Mountains!

I had a 'significant birthday' a few days ago. Birthdays are strange things, and I guess I now take the view that if we are lucky enough to celebrate one, it means that we are still alive which, I guess, is something of a plus.

However, what to do and where to go was initially something of a problem.

Frankly, I didn't fancy the idea of a party, dinner and the like this year, but really wanted to go somewhere, and well away from the tourist route, where my partner and I could both relax, enjoy a change of scene, eat good food (we are both vegetarians, which can still be an issue in the Canary Islands) and would, hopefully, provide a stimulus for my next novel.

I really didn't want to travel too far, and have the hassle of flying, nor did I want to leave the fluffies (Bella and Mackitten) in their respective kennels and cattery for too long either.

All in all, it was a tall order, but one which we resolved remarkably easily.

We finally headed to the Parador at Cruz de Tejeda, billed as being in "the heart of Gran Canaria". What a treat!

Not only did this Parador offer the most spectacular views in the most peaceful of settings, but the food was exquisite, the service remarkable, and facilities second to none.

Best of all, this Parador was only about 30 kilometres from home - although it seemed much further, because of the winding mountain roads.

The whole experience was a delightful, as well as an enriching experience that I would happily recommend to anyone, but it has set me thinking about exploring more Paradors in some of the other islands, as well as in Peninsular Spain too.

In the UK, I was a member and supporter of the National Trust, and we would often enjoy time exploring some of the magnificent buildings and gardens open to the public. In many ways, the Paradors in Spain fulfil a similar purpose - that of both preservation and accessibility.

Paradores de Turismo de España is a chain of luxury hotels that was an idea initiated by King Alfonso XIII, as a way of promoting tourism in Spain. What a good idea it was too.

It is now a profitable state-run enterprise and the hotels are situated in palaces, palaces, convents, fortresses, monasteries and other historic buildings throughout the country.

There are 93 Paradors in Spain that operate from Galicia in the north-west to Catalonia and Andalusia in the south of Spain. There are five Paradors in the Canary Islands, as well as in the Spanish cities in North Africa.

They are not particularly cheap to stay in, and prices vary according to room, region and season. However, there are often special discounts for residents (as in the Canary Islands) and other offers from time to time.

There is an equivalent organisation also operating in Portugal. These are called, the 'Pousadas de Portugal', and were founded in 1942, and I am told that these are very similar to the Spanish model.

During our stay, I spoke to one gentleman who has visited many Paradors over recent months. Both he and his wife are truly hooked on the experience.

Sadly, he has a life threatening condition, but both he and his wife are determined to make as much of the time that they have together as possible. They have the financial resources and, as a result, they visit Paradors throughout Spain for part of each month throughout the year.

It seemed to me a very good way of spending your money, if you can afford it, and to enjoy it whilst you can. As for cost, they actually compare very favourably to the price of a night in a Premier Inn in the UK, particularly if you take advantage of the special offers, and the food is much better too.

As for my next book? Yes, it did the trick and I am sure that the influence of the Parador in Cruz de Tejeda will make an appearance in a future novel.

Just 27 Crossings!

At around four kilometres long, the Avenida de Canarias in Vecindario on the island of Gran Canaria is billed as "the longest shopping street in Spain".

It is not difficult to believe such an awesome statistic, particularly when you have spent a good part of the morning trying to drive from El Doctoral, where it begins, to its end.

On a good day, I have managed the journey in about twenty minutes, but on a particularly bad day it has taken me nearly two hours. If you are the type of driver that suffers from a lack of patience, or high blood pressure, I suggest that you do not undertake the experience.

Without doubt, the Avenida de Canarias is one of the worst roads that I have driven through, and when I first arrived I used to ask why it had remained so. Surely, traffic could be diverted around Vecindario and leave this nightmare of a shopping street to take its chance with the locals?

Of course, now that I know the town, I realise that this is not the answer. Diverting traffic would immediately destroy it as a shopping centre and shoppers would instead drive to one of the many soulless shopping centres nearby and desert a once thriving shopping centre, leading it into decay and eventual ruin.

When I lived in the UK there were often complaints that, "All high streets look the same". Partly, this was true because each high street usually consisted of a Boots the Chemist, WH Smith, maybe a Debenhams, HMV, Dixons, Marks and Spencer and Woolworths (remember those?).

On my recent visit to the UK, I noticed that in many high streets, familiar stores had either closed, gone into receivership or moved into the new out-of-town shopping centre.

The previously well known shops in the high street were now replaced by empty boarded up units sporting "For Sale " and "To Rent" notices, often with some very attractive graffiti.

A general air of depression replaced what were once very busy and successful high street shopping centres. As they say, be careful what you wish for.

Back to the Canary Islands and the Avenida de Canarias. In this street there is no picturesque, historical quarter, or indeed anything vaguely historic, so cross it off your list for sightseeing.

However, what it lacks in cultural antiquities it certainly makes up for in shopping. This very busy street has all manner of shops and businesses; there is very little that you cannot purchase if you have the time, an empty credit card and the energy to wander its length.

Here, you will not find the faceless chains of clothing and electrical stores, but real shops run by real people whose livelihoods depend upon selling merchandise and services that customers want.

A mix of Spanish, Canarian, Hungarian, African, Indian, Pakistani, Chinese, Argentinean, Cuban, Polish, German and Swedish traders makes for a heady, yet healthy, mix of language, culture, faith and wares on offer.

Despite my earlier reservations, I now enjoy exploring this street. It is a place to sit in one of its many bars and restaurants and pass the time 'people watching'.

The buildings are not particularly attractive or architecturally relevant, but it is a place where real people live and work. The street employs many traffic wardens, for want of a better name.

These men and women not only allow you to park your car along the length of the street for 50 cents, but also most are friendly and polite, happy to give local information, and will often stop the traffic to help you reverse out of your parking space, if things get a little tight!

There are 27 zebra crossings from beginning to end, although I am convinced that more have been added since the last time that I counted.

This high number of zebra crossing are genuinely needed as there are always many people attempting to leap across the road, usually without looking or waiting for the traffic to stop. This is a street where, despite the heavy traffic, the pedestrian reigns supreme.

So, if you want to escape from the busy tourist centres in the south and take a glimpse at what the locals get up to during their time off work, head to Vecindario for the day.

By the way, in the Avenida de Canarias you can still get an excellent cup of coffee for just 90 cents!

Small, but beautifully formed

A special anniversary and the need for a break away recently led us to El Hierro, the smallest and most westerly of the Canary Islands.

As we live on one of the larger islands, Gran Canaria, it seemed strange to many of our friends that we should chose to spend our holiday on one of the other islands on the archipelago.

However, each of the seven inhabited Canary Islands are very different in character, scenery and tradition to each other and, being a relatively short hop away, made an ideal break.

El Hierro is within the sphere of influence of Tenerife, but is nothing like its bigger, brasher brother.

This island is quiet, very quiet and, at times, I had the feeling that maybe only half a dozen people actually lived there! In reality, it is more like 10,000 residents, but where they all hide, I really cannot say.

If you are only really interested in bars, clubs and entertainment then forget El Hierro. If you are interested in beaches with golden or white sands, then El Hierro is certainly not for you.

However, if you are interested in spectacular, long walks, a healthy sea breeze and breathtaking scenery, I can highly recommend it as a place to relax and unwind. The real world seems a very long way on El Hierro.

This island makes little allowance for the tourist. Although maps are relatively easy to find, and obtaining a guide book in English, or even Spanish, was a challenge.

Finding one in German was easier! Even the tourist information office in the island's capital, Valverde, seemed politely disinterested in tourists, and despite a visit when we first arrived in the town, it took a second visit to extract information from the tourist office that there was actually a museum in the town, quite close to the Tourist Information Office, but hidden from view and considered unworthy of a mention, it seemed!

Visitors travel to El Hierro to walk, photograph and relax. There is also considerable interest in the island's volcanic activity, which may explain why many houses appear to be boarded up.

It was fascinating to overhear groups of seismologists talking earnestly over their laptops at breakfast, examining charts and graphs of recently recorded volcanic activity.

Whilst we were on the island, a visiting party of elderly men and women visited from Lanzarote, another Canary Island, complete with their folk music group.

It was only a day visit, but they were certainly out to enjoy themselves.

I didn't really want to hire a car on this holiday, as I see quite enough of them during the year, and so we decided to make do with local buses! Needless, to say, that was our greatest mistake.

The microbus to our hotel, which also delivered newspapers, ran only once a day, and links with other routes were almost impossible to work out and it was not the most reliable of services.

A hire car is essential if you want to make the most of your holiday and see all that the island has to offer.

I left the island determined to return again one day, but next time it will be with a car and preferably a direct flight from Gran Canaria, as a stopover in Tenerife North Airport is not particularly pleasant due to the strong crosswinds!

Reminders of Home

The
Canary
Islander

A Mini in the Canaries

Did you have a love affair with a mini? No, I should clarify, I did say "with a mini" and not "in a mini" or "on a mini" - that is the stuff for a different publication. I read somewhere once that around seventy-five per cent of the British population of a certain age, have had a love affair with a mini at sometime in their lives.

I am not talking about the expensive BMW version, as superb as they are, but the original Alec Issigonis design, much loved in some of the British comedies and many other films; indeed, it was a true car of the people.

My first mini cost the princely sum of fifty pounds and, to be honest, was a little rough. The colour was supposed to be 'Snowberry White', but the exact shade had long since disappeared under layers of grime and red rust.

However, after fitting a couple of new wings, the use of a generous supply of filler and a complete paint re-spray, which my father and brother did at home, new seat covers, a padded steering wheel, a new cassette radio and a set of remould tyres, it was more or less ready to take to the road.

It certainly looked the part, although you wouldn't want to rub your hand over the bodywork - it felt like sandpaper, because Dad hadn't quite got the hang of the new spray gun and carried out the process on a windy day in a dusty Lincolnshire garage!

My mini took me from Lincolnshire to Dorset many times during my student days, and I lost count as to how many people and luggage I managed to stuff into it at any one time.

I haven't seen a 'real mini' for many years, either in the UK or in Spain, and I have to admit that I do have a real craving for one. It was the first vehicle that I had that had so much character, manoeuvrability and was, to use modern parlance, seen as exceedingly cool - at that time anyway.

On the downside, I seemed to be forever paying for new track rod ends (whatever they were), a new sub frame, as well as endless supplies of tyres and brakes. Rust was always a problem, but my Dad was always on hand with his spray gun and revised techniques, which never quite worked out, because it always felt like sandpaper, although I didn't complain.

Nowadays of course, it would never have been allowed on the road.

I spotted my first mini for many years in the Canary Islands the other day. It sat proudly on an industrial estate in Arinaga. It gleamed in the sunshine and the only thing that ruined the effect was a Honda sunshade in the front windscreen. New seat covers had been fitted and the metal work shone. It was the much-loved car of an enthusiast. The little car seemed to be beautifully cared for and was painted in a dashing shade of blue. I didn't rub my hand over the bodywork, because I thought that might lead to an arrest, but I can guarantee that it would not feel like sandpaper. How I craved to drive it!

The Grandfather Clock

I have a grandfather clock in my home. It is not antique, nor is it particularly valuable, but it is priceless to me. It is a clock made by and given to me by my father many years ago.

My father was not a carpenter by trade, but when he retired, he spent much of his leisure time in his shed at the bottom of the garden indulging his love of carpentry and wood turning. I used to tease him that it was only to get away from mother for a few hours; he would smile and say nothing.

Over a period of ten years from his retirement to his early death, my father made four grandfather clocks, one for each of my two brothers and myself and a larger one for my mother, which I have now; with the one originally given to me now passed on to my nephew for safekeeping.

My father imported high quality timepieces direct from a clockmaker in Germany, but all the cabinet work was his own design and craftsmanship.

I often look at the clock with admiration, knowing that it took many hours of painstaking, detailed craftsmanship and remembering that it was made with love. I often rub my hands over the highly polished surface, and feel the finely turned carvings.

I listen to that stealthy reassuring tick that makes our home feel a home. It makes me feel relaxed and I sense a very strong link with the past.

All expats have to make serious choices once they opt for a new life in another country. Many sell or dispose of the family possessions that they may have collected, and make a financial and personal decision to buy new furniture and household goods in their new country; this is often the cheapest and wisest option.

Others, like myself, decide to take their memories with them, in the form of books, records, personal items, family heirlooms and furniture.

This is by no means the cheapest option and I have paid a lot of money to furniture removers over the years to transport items that mean a lot to me, but are of no particular value, to my home in the Canary Islands.

Is it worth it? Yes, for me it certainly is. I look at a highly polished coffee table in our living room knowing that it was purchased at a time when money was short for the very first home that my partner and I set up together so long ago.

A pinewood dining table and chairs that have mellowed to the most beautiful golden colour over time sits in our dining room, and I remember many meals shared with family and friends; the broken and lovingly repaired swivel chair in the hallway that my brother, now deceased, sat on and broke.

I still remember the initial embarrassed silence and the subsequent guffaws of stifled laughter that is still the stuff of family memories. It still makes me smile to remember the incident.

Every Sunday evening I open the door to my grandfather clock to reset the time and to pull the heavy chain that will rewind it for another week.

Although it has been many years since it left my parents' home, that unique smell of polish and the 'family home smell' that most of us will recall from childhood in our own family homes, hit me when I open the door. For a brief moment, it is like stepping back in time; the memories come flooding back.

Was it worth the expense of transportation to an island in the Atlantic? For sentimentalists like myself, yes, it was worth every penny.

Reclaiming the flag

Visitors to the Canary Islands and Spain will notice that the flying of flags is a popular pastime. Public and government buildings, as well as many private organisations, usually proudly display three flags in the Canary Islands: the Spanish flag, the Canary Islands' flag and the flag of the European Union, and we even have another that is specific to the island of Gran Canaria.

Yes, despite the usual negativity and cynicism of many Brits, the European Union is still a popular and welcome concept in many European countries. Spain's recent victory in the European Cup has also seen a flurry of Spanish and Canarian flags adorning the homes, cars and bodies of many islanders, and has been a delight to see.

Flags are important; they are a symbol of unity and pride. Although I personally find flag waving and adorning myself in the Union flag embarrassing, I respect and admire those who do.

However, this is not the case throughout the world; we have only to look at the example of Northern Ireland, where flying a Union flag, or indeed the Republican Tricolour, is seen as provocative, and is one of the reasons why UK driving licences do not include a Union flag, but only the European Union flag, for fear of upsetting the sensitivities of some in parts of the United Kingdom.

This is a position that I understand is soon likely to change with the inclusion of both the Union flag and the European Union flag on UK driving licences, with the exception of those licences issued in Northern Ireland.

As a child, I was always taught that the national flag was called the Union Jack. In later years, we were told that this should only refer to the flag when being flown on warships, and that Union flag was the correct terminology.

I understand that the position has changed once again and we can call it whatever we wish. The idea that the Union flag should only be described as the Union Jack when flown from the bows of a warship is a relatively recent idea.

The Admiralty itself frequently referred to the flag as the Union Jack, whatever its use, and in 1902 the Admiralty declared that either name could be officially used. Parliamentary approval was given as long ago as 1908 when it was stated, "the Union Jack should be regarded as the National flag".

Therefore, I am going to return to using the original terminology that I learned at school, the Union Jack, from now on.

It recent years there has been a noticeable reduction in patriotism and pride in the UK, matched by a significant decline in 'flying the flag'.

Much of this seems to have come from the idea that displaying, waving and celebrating with the Union Jack was, in some ways, endorsing the racist and distorted views of a right wing, political party, which claimed the Union flag as the symbol of their own obnoxious organisation.

Thankfully, the balance has now been corrected and it has been good to see many ordinary people enjoying and celebrating the Queen's Jubilee, Wimbledon, Euro 2012 and the Olympic Games with their own national flag once again. The Union Jack has been reclaimed and renamed!

Hats, umbrellas, jackets, dog leads, boxes of chocolate, mugs and even slippers are now happily adorned with the Union Jack. No longer has it anything to do with allegiance with a particular political party, but is part of belonging, identity, celebration and pride.

The Union Jack has been around since 1606 and it is good to see the flag being reclaimed by ordinary people who feel pride in their country and wish to celebrate with it. Indeed, it is good to see the flags of any nation being displayed with pride anywhere in the world.

It is perfectly possible to feel pride in being English, Scottish, Welsh and Northern Irish, a member of the United Kingdom, as well as also being a good European.

Something for the Weekend, Sir?

Walking past a new hairdressing salon in a Las Palmas commercial centre made me stop and briefly retrace my steps for another look.

There was something just a little unusual about this salon and its clientele. Instead of the usual rows of salon chairs, hair dryers and display stands revealing the latest expensive hair products, were small red fire engines, delightful rocking horses, fabulous open top cars in shocking pink, and red velvet thrones fit for any aspiring King or Queen.

There were no perms or blue rinses in sight, nor were there any ladies with their hair adorned with tin foil or cling film awaiting the next stage of the colouring process. No, this establishment was strictly for kids only.

The owners of this attractive and brightly coloured salon had spotted a great business opportunity clearly aimed at those parents who have a little extra cash to spend on their children, and want them to look good.

Many children that I see here are dressed in fashionable, and I assume expensive, designer clothes and so a designer cut and style is the next obvious step.

After all, the family dog goes to the pet parlour for a cut and trim, so who can begrudge Carlos or Maria from having the best possible hair styling in a place that understands children, which is also a happy and non-threatening place to visit?

Seeing this wonderland for children, complete with a vast array of drinks, ice creams, sweets and designer accessories, made me think back to my own childhood and the times that I dreaded going for a haircut at the barbers in the Lincolnshire village where I lived.

How I hated visiting Potter's, with its heavy door, dark wood panelled walls and strange smells. The queues of grumpy, smelly old men, many of whom were smoking cigarettes or pipes, sat on wooden benches waiting their turn for a shave or haircut.

The heady, sickly smell of Brylcreem, combined with tobacco smoke made for a heady, vomit-inducing mix for a young child.

It was always a mixed blessing when my turn finally came, and I was beckoned forward and strapped into what look like a dentist's chair and shrouded in a huge white sheet.

Mr Potter continued talking to the smelly, grumpy old men whilst he operated, cut and fiddled with my hair with his enormous pair of scissors and comb. Mr Potter was probably a very nice man, but as he never spoke to me, I really cannot say for sure. The final insult was the thick globule of that ghastly, sticky Brylcreem ladled out of its white pot into my hair before I escaped from the chair and was directed to a bench to wait until someone came to collect me.

The strange thing is that I cannot remember being taken or collected; I just remember being there.

It is a memory that haunts me to this day and one of the reasons why, as soon as I became responsible for my own hairdressing actions, I refused to set foot in another barber's shop, and much preferred unisex salons.

Well, at least they had no Brylcreem on the premises! This was until a few weeks ago when my own delightful hairdresser was on holiday and I needed a quick cut. I foolishly entered a barber's shop in the town where I live.

As I walked inside the dark panelled shop, memories came flooding back of troubled times long gone. Along the walls were seated a similar group of smelly, grumpy old men sitting on wooden benches waiting their turn that I remembered so well.

Two 'dentists' chairs filled the far side of the room, whilst two barbers in white coats cut, poked and prodded their victims' hair with large scissors. I made my excuses and swiftly fled to the nearest bar for a coffee and brandy.

Thinking about the new kid's salon in Las Palmas, with Carlos sitting in the fire engine and Maria on the horse eating sweets and listening to music that they liked, made me realise just how lucky they were. If I had been them, I would have chosen the shocking pink sports car!

You look well!

Many of us have words or phrases that make us cringe when we hear them. For me, it is usually the American misinterpretation of the English language, as I see it anyway.

I often think that there is no such thing as American English, and that English used in the USA should simply be called 'American' and have done with it, leaving 'English' as the very distinct form of English spoken in England!

Although I love most Americans, maybe with the exception of George Bush and Sarah Palin, why use the word 'fall' when you mean 'Autumn', 'semester' when you simply mean 'term'?

As for the use of the word 'cellphone', when we simply mean 'mobile', words fail me. For that matter, why do pupils in the USA 'graduate' and receive a cap, gown and diploma when they simply leave infant school? I could go on, but I won't!

When I make a rare visit to relatives back in Lincolnshire in the UK, I am usually greeted with the welcome "You look well!"

How I hate this! It actually shows no concern whatsoever about my general state of health, or recognition of my healthy Canarian tan; it simply means, "You look fat" or "You've put on weight". I grit my teeth and smile a benign smile.

My well meaning and much-looked-forward-to visit tends to go rapidly downhill from that point onwards.

Maybe it is the Lincolnshire equivalent of a deeply resonating "eeee" that many Canarians and Spanish utter when they are desperately trying to think of something to say when responding to a phone call, or the "errr" sound, much loved and used by the British, as a way of playing for time and before entering into meaningful conversation.

I guess they are simply 'thinking sounds'.

I also detest the use of current expressions such as "growing a business", which, if you think about it, is complete nonsense, but fill many chapters of some of the American "How to succeed in business" management theory books.

However, for me, one of the worst expressions used in recent times is the use of the word "product" when referring to some kind of financial service.

This is a very dangerous expression and is, in my view, one of the main reasons why we have entered into an economic downturn. I was taught at school that a product is "something that is produced by labour or effort".

Over recent years, I have failed to see why the banks' latest packaging of an over-priced bank account or a new financial service, designed to ease away as much cash from my pocket as it can, could be in any way be seen as a product.

Maybe, over the years the use of the word 'product' has lulled us into a false sense of security: we think we are actually producing something, when in reality we are producing nothing at all.

Maybe it is akin to the story of 'The Emperor's new clothes", when the little boy declared to the Emperor, who was busily flaunting his new gear, that actually he was naked and was wearing no clothes at all. Well, that is part of my explanation for the financial crash!

I am sure that we all have words and expressions that irritate us. If you have a favourite one, do please let me know.

It's an island thing

I have always loved islands. Maybe it was reading just too much Robinson Crusoe, Enid Blyton's 'Five on a Treasure Island' and other stories about islands that inspired me, but I always knew that one day I would live on an island.

Maybe it was that first glimpse of the magical and mysterious Brownsea Island pointed out to me by my elderly great aunt.

We could only view it through binoculars from Poole Harbour in Dorset, because, in those days, as my great aunt explained, it was inhabited by an old witch and her elderly manservant, and they cooked and ate all newcomers to the island.

Animals, birds and insects that lived there were special and unique to that special place. Indeed, the giant ants could eat people alive.

As I discovered many years later whilst accompanying classes of schoolchildren to the island, she was partly right about the giant ants! Great Aunt Gertie did have a vivid imagination, but it was the stuff of inspiration.

For many years I thought that my eventual island destination would be the Isle of Wight.

Career opportunities often seemed to lead me there, and on one occasion it was the dreadful realisation that I was about to be offered a job that I didn't really want, that made me flee the island at 5.00am one morning and well before the final interview, and I didn't return for many years.

We visited the Scilly Islands - a delightful destination, but I soon realised that the rusting bath tub, which the islanders call a ferry, was a nightmare, and after one terrible voyage with myself and other passengers vomiting for most of the journey, I flew back to the mainland by helicopter realising that I could never attempt that journey by boat ever again, let alone live there.

We spent many glorious summers exploring islands around the UK and beyond. We tasted delicious malt whiskies on the Isles of Skye and Islay, exploring the Outer Hebrides, avoiding tweed jackets in Harris and Lewis, as well as tasting the relative decadence of Orkney and Shetland.

Islands as diverse as Majorca, Cyprus, Ibiza and Madeira were also visited, but although wonderful in their own unique ways, none seemed to inspire me as a possible home for the future.

That is until we visited the Canary Islands in general, and Gran Canaria in particular. I knew then that this would be home and found myself gripping the handrail and forcing myself up the steps of the plane going home at the end of our first visit. I was determined to return again one day.

So what is so special about islands? It is a difficult one to answer, because people are inspired in many different ways. Maybe it is the feeling of being part of a small community, never being far from the sea, or the reminder of a primitive form of survival instinct.

Maybe it is just that feeling of "Getting away from it all", although critics of this view will quickly point out that this can be difficult to achieve on islands such as Tenerife, and parts of Gran Canaria and Lanzarote! If you really do want to get away from it all, I suggest heading to El Hierro, La Gomera or La Palma instead!

An elderly friend visited a few days ago. "I could never live on an island," she declared loudly after critically peering out to sea. What do you do for shopping? You have only got one small shop," she asked.

"We have many good local shops nearby, and you can get anything in Las Palmas, the seventh largest city in Spain," I replied.

"It must be so difficult to get off the island in an emergency?" she frowned.

"Not really, after all Las Palmas airport is the third largest in Spain. Flights are always available, but the fares vary depending upon demand."

"I would need still need to be in Europe, because of the health service".

"The Canary Islands are part of Europe and offer some of the best medical treatment available anyway. Indeed, patients are often flown to Las Palmas from the Peninsular for specialist treatment."

"Hmm, well, I still wouldn't like to live in an island..." she mumbled.

Great, I thought. I am so pleased you are not going to move here. Intending islanders need to be committed to island life and be aware of the disadvantages, as well as the advantages.

Islands are rather like Marmite, Blackpool or Benidorm. You either love them or hate them.

Tulip Heads and Cabbage Fields

Life in the Canary Islands and Spain always seems to be punctuated by amazing Carnivals and enthusiastic Fiestas. There are just so many, with each town and village having their own special patron saint and accompanying fiesta days (or weeks, in some cases!); sometimes it is hard to keep up with them.

I love to see, hear and take part in them if I can. It is wonderful to see Canarian children dressed in traditional costume, singing and dancing, with their parents and friends enjoying the warmth of the day until late evening or, more usually, early morning.

I am sure that these early experiences, traditions and social activities have a considerable influence upon the sense of belonging, community spirit and working together that is so important for a well-balanced life.

During the recent fiesta in my own village, I began to reflect and contrast what I was seeing with some of my own childhood experiences.

I was born and grew up in fenland Lincolnshire which, to be frank, was never my favourite place. A landscape of endless fields growing the same crop in a tree-less and hedge-less landscape, without a hill in sight, and usually accompanied by a grey sky was simply not for me.

I felt from a very early age that I was in the wrong place and I knew that one day I would have to escape.

However, in fairness, I also know many people who, if not exactly loving it, tolerated it as a place where they grew up, have many happy memories, and I respect their views. However, sadly, that was not the case for me.

One overpowering memory that I still have, in more ways than one, is the overwhelming smell of rotting cabbages at certain times of the year, often combined with the sweet, sickly smell of sugar beet being processed in the local beet factory.

It was a strange and heady combination if the wind was in the wrong direction. The fertile land of South Lincolnshire is, of course, where farmers grow much of the nation's crops, and a very good job they make of it too.

However, endless fields of cabbages, cauliflowers and potatoes were never quite my thing, and I always seemed to be surrounded by fields emitting the bad stench of rotting cabbages and cauliflowers.

How I longed to escape from that place. I guess this is when I started to dream about islands.

In contrast, some fields were dedicated to the growing of tulip bulbs. In springtime, the usual bland landscape that haunted me as a child would burst into life with thousands upon thousands of tulips.

Each field would specialise in one particular variety and colour; sparkling yellows, vivid reds, variegated varieties, and even blood red or almost black varieties.

On my journey to and from school each day, the school bus would weave its way through fields of colour, much like large patches of raw, vivid colour on an artist's palette. It lifted my spirits tremendously, and was such a change from cabbages.

The tulips were, of course, grown for their bulbs and not for their flowers, and so the time would come when all the flowers were beheaded and carted off in huge trucks to the nearest compost heap.

This would allow the bulbs to grow, divide and make healthy profits for the farmers. Indeed, this part of Lincolnshire was called Holland, and was reclaimed land from the Wash with a flower and bulb industry similar to its neighbour, the Netherlands, which was just a short hop across the North Sea.

Fortunately, imaginative people began to realise that the tulip heads could in themselves still be quite useful, and the beginnings of a kind of Carnival began to grow in my home town of Spalding.

Large floats, sponsored by local businesses and large companies, were decorated with tulip heads. Amazing, spectacular creations from tulip heads, now in the form of floats, arrived each year as local groups and businesses tried to outdo their rivals.

A huge procession would take place through the town and 'The Tulip Parade' became known worldwide as a spectacular event, which was well worth including on the tourist map. There was even a 'Tulip Queen', suitably crowned, who rode through the town in her carriage of tulips.

The floats would then be on show for the general public to admire for several days until the heads finally died and all would be forgotten for another year.

For me, and others like me, those few days each year were heaven sent during a time when my world seemed to be full of cabbages.

Many years later, when I was working as a school inspector, I was dispatched to Lincolnshire for a week to inspect a school.

I arrived at the motel late at night and so was unsure of my immediate surroundings. When I awoke the following morning, I was once again greeted with that familiar smell, the overpowering smell of rotting cabbages!

Faith, Politics and Belief

The
Canary
Islander

The Euro Game

It was a hot, sunny day and the boys and girls in the village school were enjoying their lunchtime games as usual in the schoolyard. However, today, tempers seemed a little more frayed than usual during this particular ball game.

I watched the children closely for some time anticipating that the dinner lady who was supervising would have to step in and bring the game to an abrupt end, intervening with the usual talk about sporting behaviour and "it's not the winning, it's the playing" reminder that teachers and dinner ladies are so good at repeating.

I then noticed one girl from my class, Sally, was frowning and concentrating hard. Sally was a born leader; she had presence, and although not always liked by her classmates, she would be the one to lead and organise whenever anything needed doing. She was barking instructions to one very agile small boy, Peter, who seemed to pop up all over the playground at the same time from nowhere.

Peter was a very happy little boy, friendly to everyone and always happy to help out, yet he had a quiet determination that could bring about revolution if he wished; such was his charisma. Sally and Peter working together brought about a special kind of teamwork, that initially seemed unlikely, but now appeared to be working. Although the shouting and arguments continued, there now seemed to be order and a plan in their game.

Suddenly, there was a cry from Charles. Charles looked angry as the ball bounced off his back. His face was red and he angrily dived towards the ball, which he grabbed and then stood glaring at the others. His teammates shouted for him to pass the ball.

He looked defiant and his face was now filling with tears. Charles placed the ball under his arm, marched off the playground with the ball and back into the school building. He bit his bottom lip angrily and slammed the door

behind him. For a few seconds, the rest of the children stood and watched with their mouths open, wondering what all the fuss was about.

Sally looked angry as she strode off the playground and found another ball in the sports shed. She returned to the playground and threw the ball to Peter who deftly caught it and threw it back into the game. The children cheered as the game continued at a pace that was faster and more focussed than before.

Before I returned into the school building, I caught a glimpse of Charles, his tear stained face watching the game alone from the classroom window.

The recent meeting of leaders in Paris, designed to discuss the future of the Euro and Britain's participation in amending its financial rules, reminded me of a children's game in a Dorset rural primary school some years ago.

Does one size fit all?

I still enjoy reading and listening to UK news. However, I do find it irritating to hear economists and financial 'experts' (In the UK they are usually anti EU and anti euro) including Portugal, Italy and Spain in any discussion about the euro crisis and Greece.

I hear Spain condemned in similar terms as Greece in the same breath, almost as if it is an extension of the same problem.

Most UK financial 'experts' appear to be anti European and certainly anti euro, and the arrogance of the "we told you the euro would be a disaster" brigade is breathtaking, particularly as many of us remember those very same pundits recommending the UK's entry to the eurozone some years ago.

Yes, hindsight is indeed a wonderful thing.

Spain's problems, and therefore the cure, are very different from those of Greece, as well as Italy, Ireland and Portugal.

Spain has been an enthusiastic member of the European Union from its very beginning, and most Spanish people readily accept that the highly successful transition from the dictatorship of General Franco to a modern democratic state in a short period of time has been largely due to the support and encouragement from the EU.

Most of the eurozone's problems relate to excessive borrowing by governments who were ineffective in managing their economies.

Greece, for instance, was unable to control its spending, and produced figures that were simply not true when applying to join the eurozone. Portugal spent and borrowed too much. Italy also had too much debt stemming from overspending in the 1970s and 1980s.

Believe it or not, Spain has been a model European state, very similar in approach to Germany. Germany had wisely insisted upon including a 'stability pact', which was designed to ensure that governments inside the eurozone would organise their finances sensibly.

If a country wished to join the eurozone, a condition of entry was that their debts should be no more than 60% of their GDP. However, this condition was quietly forgotten at the beginning, because Germany would not have qualified for entry to the eurozone, because its debts were too high; this was the eurozone's first big mistake.

The stability pact itself was not implemented, because Germany broke the annual borrowing limit each year from 2002 to 2005. However, the Spanish government ran a balanced budget, with borrowing at zero every year until the 2008 financial crisis.

Spain's debt ratio fell and its economy grew rapidly, whilst Germany's debt continued to rise. This was hardly a Greece scenario.

Spain now faces a difficult economic dilemma, because interest rates reduced to the lower levels operating in Germany when it joined the eurozone.

Although the Spanish government resisted the temptation of low interest loans, most ordinary Spanish people did not, and the country enjoyed a long economic boom, accompanied by a housing bubble, as Spanish families obtained larger mortgages, encouraged by some banks with less than rigorous lending policies; a problem that was also echoed in the UK.

House prices increased by 44% between 2004 and 2008, yet now have fallen.

Spanish workers earned more and spent more during the years of growth, which helped to increase the government's finances from taxation, yet also helped to increase Spanish wages to uncompetitive levels, when compared with workers in Germany.

Its construction sector, which became bloated during the building boom, also collapsed.

Currently, households are attempting to reduce their spending, as they struggle to repay their mortgages and financial debts.

Unemployment has increased rapidly, with 50 per cent of under 25-year-olds currently out of work.

Surprisingly, unlike Greece, the Spanish government has relatively little debt, but now has to borrow to cover the shortfall left by a collapse in tax revenues and a rise in unemployment benefits during the downturn.

Banks too are exposed to the collapse of the housing market due to their mortgage debts, which makes financial markets cautious about lending to Spain.

It is also well worth remembering that, unlike Greece, Spain is the EU's fourth largest economy and the twelfth largest in the world.

The country still maintains a large and strong industrial base; for example, it manufactures cars, heavy machinery, washing machines and refrigerators. Agricultural, fish and wine products continue to find a ready market within other countries of the EU, traditional links with South America, as well as newly established markets in China and India. Spain's tourism industry continues to boom and is still the largest within the European Union.

Spain has much going for it, and it has very different issues, as well as possibilities, to those of Greece and other eurozone economies. Wise economists, who have knowledge of the country, are slowly realising that Spain requires a different solution to its problems, and a gradual recognition that one size does not fit all. Spain can reform itself, but the support of its European partners is essential for it to succeed. The one common factor with Greece is that there is a limit to how much pain its people can take.

Bankers Go Bananas

I thought that I recognised the voice over the underground station's speaker system; it sounded familiar, but I couldn't quite place it. The doors slid silently to a close as I sat in the immaculate carriage and sped my way to Canary Wharf.

Many years had passed since I last made the journey to this centre of the UK's banking industry and I was curious to see how it had developed.

It was a strange day to visit, as the Barclays interest rate scandal had just been announced, and it was clear that heads would soon roll.

I was also curious, since many years ago when the Thatcher government was busily telling UK citizens that they should all be shareholders, my building society account had been gobbled up by the bank that was now causing so much grief to Government and bankers alike, and was now based in Canary Wharf.

It was a delicious form of irony, as it seemed that a number of wayward chickens were about to come home to roost.

I felt a special affinity to this part of London. The Canary Islands are now my home and I am well aware of the banana trade and the impact that it made upon Canary Wharf.

Bananas from the Canary Islands were once unloaded right in the centre of what is now London's vibrant financial district, which takes its name from the No. 10 Warehouse of the South Quay Import Dock, built in 1952 for the Canary Islands' fruit trade.

This grey glass and steel paradise proudly retains the name Canary Wharf to this day.

The train slid into the bland and clinical station. I stepped out of the concrete, stainless steel and glass structure, relieved to smell relatively fresh air once again.

It was a grey, depressing day and the grey steel, concrete and glass structures that loomed around me seemed to be more intimidating than the last time that I had visited.

Apart from a few tourists holding their Union flag umbrellas, the place seemed abandoned. I wandered alongside the river for a while, marvelling at the huge number of sushi bars, coffee shops and fast food restaurants; most were empty.

At exactly midday, thousands of ant-like creatures appeared from the grey, glass and steel towers. I have never seen so many suits gathered in one place at one time before.

The ant-like creatures swept into the sushi bars, coffee shops and fast food restaurants devouring anything in sight. I wandered into one of the many high tech shopping centres; glass doors silently opening and closing behind me.

Suit clad ants sped in all directions carrying what seemed to be an obligatory cup of coffee in a plastic mug in one hand, and a mobile phone clamped in the other. Expressionless faces swept by me as they darted around the high tech paradise.

I sat inside one of the many coffee shops sipping my coffee, watching these expressionless faces. Many were deep in conversation on their mobiles, or peering into the screens of laptops, mobiles and tablets; few were talking to each other.

The enormous screens in the coffee bar continued to beam endless streams of trading figures and financial statistics, and transfixed anxious faces by its magical, seductive power.

By mid afternoon, the 'ants' had all but disappeared back into their grey steel and glass towers, the anxious chattering into handsets silenced, busy cafe bars, restaurants and sushi bars emptied and the streets were deserted once again.

I returned to the station, anxious to return to what I regarded as civilisation. I was troubled by what I had seen and experienced. It was not a happy place; it reminded me of a book that I had read long ago, but couldn't quite remember.

A familiar voice boomed around the station once again. It was slightly humorous, with a hint of self-deprecation, yet tinged with just a hint of a threat.

Yes, the book was 1984 and I suddenly realised that I had briefly entered the Orwellian nightmare. I now recognised the voice of Big Brother - it was the voice of Boris Johnson, the Mayor of London.

Quakers in the Canaries

My mother warned me long ago not to talk about politics, sex or religion at the dinner table. I think to this, she would have added not talking about vegetarianism at a barbecue.

All these subjects appear to be off limits in polite company, and maybe for good reason as outspoken, individual views may offend, lead to disagreement, argument or, indeed, revolution.

In this chapter, I am going to break the rule about religion, not I might add because I wish to cause offence, but because I know that it is an issue that troubles many expats, as well as being an issue that I have only recently become aware of.

If talking about God and faith isn't quite your thing, please accept my apologies and skip to the next chapter.

My personal faith is very simple. I believe in a loving God, Creator, or whatever you wish to call Him (or Her). I have a deep faith, but dislike organised religion. I don't feel the need for vicars, ministers, priests, Pope's, Imams and the like, because I wish to have a direct relationship with my God.

I don't feel the need to use rosary beads, sing hymns and psalms, and chant meaningless phrases, because I believe that my God understands and tolerates me just as I am. I feel uncomfortable in extravagant cold and underused church buildings that often ignore the needs of their communities.

I dislike the hoarding and display of valuable paintings, gold and silver plate, cups and chalices, which I regard as fripperies and largely irrelevant. However, I do like stained glass windows, which make me think and deepen my faith.

I don't like the smell of incense, which makes me sneeze, nor do I have the urge to listen to dozens of choirboys singing in their high pitched, yet beautiful, voices; I know that most would much rather be elsewhere on an early Sunday morning.

Despite my personal views, I fully accept that many people value and appreciate the traditions and trappings of organised religion. Many find priests, vicars and ministers invaluable and many dedicate their lives to giving high quality leadership, support and care to their parishioners.

This is fair enough, as long as the views of the organised Church do not disrespect, disturb or ignore the values or rights of others. Much of this is, of course, about tolerance and recognition of the needs and views of others in a civilised society.

Many years ago, my partner and I became Quakers. Without going into too much detail here, Quakers hold simple beliefs based around simple truths. There are no priests, ministers and Popes. Church buildings (called Meeting Houses) are simple, welcoming places and are often used for other purposes by the local community.

There is no fixed order for the service; indeed, there is no service as such. There are usually no hymns, no prayer books or psalms. Quakers meet in silence for an hour; it is a time for peace and meditation and a time for people to relate to their own God.

Occasionally, a member may share a thought or an idea with the meeting. These thoughts that are shared with the Meeting are often reflective and thoughtful, yet rarely dull. Although Quaker meetings are held in silence, there is plenty of opportunity for laughter, discussion and gossip afterwards over coffee!

After attending many churches over the years, I immediately felt comfortable when I walked through the door of a Meeting House in the UK. This is one of the things that I do miss as an expat.

Over time, I have come to realise that I can worship anywhere. The area by the sea where I walk Bella, our dog, each day is my Church. My God hears me when I talk and explain my problems, share my successes, ask for forgiveness and ask for advice.

My silent prayers are accompanied by the sounds of an often, stormy sea or wind. My church has no walls, stained glass windows or ornate crosses - just a simple backdrop of a blue sky, a few fluffy white clouds, and some seabirds and lizards for company.

It is always good to go home. My partner, David, and myself experienced just that feeling recently when we visited our Bournemouth Quaker 'home'.

For the last ten years, we have lived and worked in Spain's Costa Blanca and now the Canary Islands. Although we love our Canary Island's home, I guess nothing is ever perfect, and we do miss our friends and family in the UK and the opportunity to attend meeting.

There are relatively few Quakers in Spain, and none that we are aware of living on the island where we live. I occasionally receive emails and letters from visiting Quakers, usually from the USA, asking for a contact or meeting house in the country, and it is sometimes difficult to assist, as people change and move on.

David and I often crave the opportunity to worship with like-minded people, but we have been fortunate in being welcomed in meeting houses in Dublin, Lincolnshire and Devon, whilst visiting family and friends.

The sun beamed through the tall windows of the meeting room. We had arrived early to make the most of our brief visit. As we sat in silence, Friends slipped into the room and sat down.

Several who remembered us from ten years earlier, looked surprised and warmly acknowledged us, whilst others we had not seen before nodded and smiled. There were many new faces and it was good to see that the overall attendance seemed to have increased.

Superficially, some things had changed, the washroom had been refurbished, areas redecorated and floors looked even more highly polished than I recall.

A candle replaced the fresh flowers that were usually placed on the central table, and there was now even an automatic door to the front entrance. However, the seats were still just as uncomfortable as I remember.

Despite the physical changes, the many new faces and the absence of many older friends, the atmosphere remained as supportive, warm and loving as we remembered. Although Quakers usually worship in silence, they certainly make up for it over coffee and can chatter with the best of them.

We renewed acquaintance with many members from the past, as well as meeting many new members and attenders. It was a happy and emotional visit and our only regret was that we could not stay longer for lunch.

Even though we now live in the Canary Islands, we are still members of the Bournemouth Meeting. We receive the newsletter and other information each month, as we have for the last ten years, and this is always much appreciated. During difficult times we have received letters of support from Friends.

David and I still worship most Sundays, at 10.30am to feel part of the Bournemouth Meeting, even though we are many miles away. We have our quiet hour, when sometimes David plays reflective music on the keyboard. Although we are usually only two, we recall these words of Jesus:

"For where two or three are gathered together in my name, there am I in the midst of them."

As usual, our time in the UK was a manic one. Visiting friends and family, book events and a school visit meant that our time was limited and we had to be on our way. Thank you Bournemouth Meeting; we hope it will not be too long before we visit again.

The Conservatory Government

Despite the seriousness of the current recession, I have been amused and irritated by the constant references to the relaxation of rules for the building of conservatories in the UK.

Presumably the rules were originally introduced for a good reason and it seems a little unwise to many people to suddenly abandon them.

It is as if suddenly allowing a huge conservatory to be built in the back garden of a semi in Huddersfield, without planning permission, will transform the nation's economy.

Now, I know it is easy to be cynical at such times, and I like conservatories as much as the next person, but maybe the emphasis upon conservatories may give the wrong idea about priorities to the struggling masses? It is just a thought.

We don't have the conservatory problem in the Canary Islands and much of Spain. If we are fortunate, our homes have a roof terrace to sit on, dry washing on, plant a few tubs, or maybe, if it is large enough, to have a barbecue.

It is often amusing to watch the newly arrived expat, when faced with a glorious roof terrace, to almost immediately have it covered with glazed roof panels!

I can see that it will provide an additional room, as well as being a lovely garden room to sit in on the occasional cool, windy day, but such home improvements tend to ignore the intense heat that we enjoy for much of the year.

What originally seemed an excellent idea in providing additional covered space, quickly turns into a nightmare of searing heat, which becomes an oven if entering the room for more than half a minute.

Modifications are then made to the offending roof panels, ranging from shading, or expensive blinds, painting or covering the outside of the glass panels with reflective paint, installing electric opening or sliding roof panels, covering it with a solid roof, or removing the complete installation.

How Canarian builders must snigger when they receive their next order from a well-intentioned expat to create a sun room!

Maybe the Conservatory Government should consider this possibility when developing recession busting policies; it would suddenly create huge additional demand for building work across the nation.

On a more serious note, Canarian and Spanish families traditionally look after the elderly members of their families.

Unlike the UK, there are few private residential homes in the country, other than those run by holy orders, which may not be everyone's idea of having a good time in old age.

It is therefore a Canarian's first priority, when moving into a new home with a terrace or balcony, to immediately build a solid roof and turn it into a bedroom for Granny, with or without planning permission.

As a result, some of the structures look rather strange and I feel for all the Grannies on the island when there is excessive wind or heavy rain. Granny, in turn, often will look after the kids, Mum and Dad can go out to work with no childcare concerns, and so all the family benefits from this system of in-house Granny care.

So my advice to the Conservatory Government and the Chancellor of the Exchequer in the UK, for what it is worth, is to allow the building of everything anywhere, with little or no planning permission, to create as many homes in as many nooks and crannies as possible, especially for the nation's Grannies.

This will create jobs for builders, solve the Granny housing crisis, reduce the cost of care for Grannies, provide additional childcare, and allow all Mums and Dads to go out to work.

As a bonus, it will provide additional work for insurance companies and lawyers when dealing with insurance claims for collapsed roofs, as well as compensation for infringement of light and airspace claims from the folks next door. The nation's economy will boom and it will be the end of the recession. Only then will the UK have a true Conservatory Government.

Food, Drink and Health

The
Canary
Islander

A decent cup of coffee

In a previous 'Twitter' I referred to a high quality coffee grown in Gran Canaria and now marketed in a number of European countries as a premium product. Now it seems that another type of coffee, grown in the Canary Islands, will shortly enter the market and this time it is made from pistachio nuts.

A decent cup of coffee is, for me, an essential part of each morning. I don't think I have ever been disappointed with a cup of coffee in Spain and the Canary Islands. However, the soup bowls full of the stuff in the UK's many overpriced 'Costa Lottee' chains invariably make both my stomach and wallet churn.

Even though I like a cup of good coffee in the morning, I am careful not to drink too many and reluctantly settle for a cup of decaffeinated coffee later in the evening, although I am not that keen on the taste.

I know that coffee with a high caffeine content significantly reduces the quality of sleep and is best avoided late at night; however, late evening meals and the desire for a good cup of coffee and a decent brandy to round off a good meal makes for a difficult choice, and I easily succumb to temptation.

Maybe the Canary Islands have an answer? It seems that coffee made from pistachio nuts can be used to make a healthier, caffeine-free alternative to coffee, as well as being a genuine alternative that actually tastes like coffee.

Coffee manufacturers have been searching for a good stimulant-free alternative to coffee that maintains the flavour, but without the kick of real coffee.

The fruit of Pistacia terebinthus (terebinth and turpentine tree), a deciduous tree that grows to a height of more than 30 feet is native to the Canary Islands, as well as Morocco, Turkey and Greece, and produces red to black coloured fruit, and scientists claim that if these are carefully roasted they will produce a drink that has the same flavour as coffee, but without the high. One added bonus for producers is that this fruit is significantly cheaper than the real thing.

As well as producing a sap that is a source of turpentine, the tree produces a special type of pistachio nut that has the same chemical "signature" as real coffee, and with the same taste and aroma. When roasted, there is a change in the chemical profile similar to that when coffee beans are roasted.

Coffee experts report that the new "healthy coffee" is brewed in the same way as Turkish coffee, and produces a dark brown, rich coffee with a nutty and chocolate smell.

However, the new product is not as successful in producing espresso coffee, which may restrict its marketing potential to the trendy coffee bars, because the roasted nuts turn into a less than attractive gunge that prevents water from running through the product.

It will be interesting to see what happens, but I hope that once again, it proves that when it comes to a decent cup of coffee, it is hard to beat the Canary Islands.

The World Cradle of Rum

Visitors to the Canary Islands may remember that at the end of a good meal in a local restaurant, and before the bill arrives, they are presented with a 'shot' - a small glass of liqueur to round off a good meal.

This 'shot' is presented as a 'on the house' gesture of gratitude from the restaurant for visiting, with the hope that you will visit again, as well as remembering to leave a tip before you leave.

This 'shot' is often a local Canarian Honey Rum, known as Ron Miel, which is made from a centuries old tradition of blending aged rum and honey. It is a sweet drink, but not as sweet as you might at first think, and certainly not as sickly to the taste as some liqueurs.

It also includes a remarkable 'kick' if you drink too many, and it may also be wise not to accept your 'shot' if you are the driver!

It is often forgotten that when you speak about rum, you are talking about the Canary Islands; the two are intertwined. Many rum connoisseurs describe the Canary Islands as the 'World Cradle of Rum', where this beautiful spirit is made by combining a centuries old tradition with the superb quality of locally produced raw materials.

White rum, banana rum, toffee rum, chocolate cream, coco-pineapple and coffee rum are just some of the many varieties available although, personally, I am rather fond of the banana variety!

So how is Honey Rum made? Seven-year-old rum is blended with natural honey from the Canary Islands, which create a natural combination of flavour. It may be enjoyed on its own, or you can ruin it by mixing it into a range of mixed drinks and cocktails.

Although mixing may not be for the rum connoisseur, it is fair to say that Honey Rum does an excellent job as a natural substitute for man-made sugars and liqueurs.

One company that produces honey rum is Distillery Arehucus, which has recently proudly announced that it is shipping and selling its traditional 'Ron Miel de Canarias' to the USA. Distillery Arehucas is a fourth generation family owned business, which produces a range of world class rums and is the official supplier to the Spanish Royal family, so it can't be bad!

Traditional methods of production and quality are still used at the distillery, a local family business, which began rum production 125 years ago, and currently produces around 1.5 million litres each year. It is a fair bet that if you have already tried honey rum, or one of its sister flavours, it may well have been one produced by Distillery Arehucas, since they have around 50 per cent of the market share in honey rum on the islands and Europe.

The new export to the USA, as well as designed to tickle the American palette, also has an interesting history, with established links to the sugar cane industry, rum production and the USA.

All four voyages of Christopher Columbus, or Cristobal Colon as they like to call him over here, departed from the Canary Islands to the New World, and the first sugar canes planted in America left from the Canary islands bound for the West Indies in the second voyage of Christopher Columbus, in 1493.

Very appropriately, the current stock of sugar cane currently growing in the West Indies is originally from the Canary Islands.

Personally, I am not a great lover of cocktails, and to use Ron Miel as a mixer in any drink would be, in my view, dangerously close to sacrilege. My personal favourite is the banana variety, and I am sure that you will have great enjoyment trying out the range of Ron Miel!

Besides, it may also be regarded as almost medicinal, as it is great for soothing sore throats, so do keep a bottle in your medicine cabinet, just in case!

Most expats will find themselves frequently travelling to and from their countries of origin.

Whether it is visiting family and friends, or the occasional flight back to the UK for business or maybe a shopping trip, most expats will find themselves spending hours on the Internet attempting to find the best value flights.

The joy of finding a so called 'cheap flight' from one of the not so cheap low cost airlines is often tempered by a plethora of additional charges for luggage, taxes and credit card surcharges.

There is also a variety of other available options, such as a once in a lifetime opportunity to purchase a cabin bag that is guaranteed to be allowed on board, paying an optional charge for the joy of sitting together as a couple or family, extra leg room, or maybe for an in-flight meal.

How about insurance, a hotel room, or maybe car hire? By the time would-be travellers have booked their flights, most are just relieved to have reached the end of the process and no longer care about the detail!

I am one of those rare species of traveller who actually enjoys eating airline food. For years I have remained silent whilst my fellow travellers sneered and complained about the contents of the plastic food tray, lovingly presented to them by beaming and mostly efficient airline stewards and stewardesses.

Mostly, my fellow passengers consumed the offerings grudgingly, but a few trays remained uneaten. Incidentally, who remembers the days when the meal ended with the serving of a steaming hot damp cloth, delicately served with a pair of serving tongs from a silver tray? Nice touch, but a little pointless, I felt.

Some passengers would decline their meals with a meaningful grunt, and turn their backs upon the offending tray that was offered to them. They were making a statement about something or other, and anyway, they had a less than fresh ham and cheese sandwich stuffed somewhere about their person, which would offer them a modicum of comfort during the serving of these culinary delicacies.

Meanwhile, the rest of us were enjoying the latest hot food offering, whilst flying at a height 30,000 odd feet, and very good it was too.

I could never understand the complaints, or the endless jokes that the in-flight meal caused. Indeed, the flying food tray became the butt of many aspiring comedians. Maybe I just didn't notice, had such a boring and unappetising diet in my out-of-the-air life, or maybe it was because I am a vegetarian and always ordered the vegetarian option.

Whatever it was, my veggie meal often used to elicit admiring glances from fellow passengers or comments of "that looks tasty" as they peered into my Mediterranean casserole or mushroom omelette.

All this of course was when the airline meal was included in the price of the ticket. That, and the obligatory ancient cartoon on tiny screens were included as part of the package deal; there was simply no choice.

The in-flight meal then became an easy target for many Brits, being a cynical lot at the best of times, to ridicule something that was actually rather good. How I missed its sudden demise!

The in-flight meal was replaced by a sad selection of filled rolls, designer paninis and expensive crisps, and the total outlay often cost far in excess of an in-flight meal. However, some of the more sensible airlines continued to offer in-flight meals, but usually only as an optional extra.

In-flight meals then became the province of designer TV chefs to have their say, and produce meals worthy of launching or ending a holiday in the sun, rather than the product of ex-school cooks who couldn't quite hack it in airline catering departments, and were tucked away on an industrial estate somewhere.

Nowadays, I much prefer to book flights with airlines that offer this option, as well as a booked seat, as I prefer this to the gallop across the tarmac and the purchase of a packet of nuts from a certain Irish airline, with a "catch them out if we can" attitude on its website.

As I write this, I have just finished my in-flight meal. It was a delicious gnocchi with butternut squash, strawberry cheesecake, cheese and biscuits, coffee and a chocolate mint, and very good it was too. Interestingly, over half of the passengers on my flight had opted to purchase the in-flight meal, albeit I guess most opted for the beef or chicken options.

The creator of this particular in-flight meal chef promised "Good satisfying comfort food, made with quality ingredients", which it certainly was.

It is now all about personal choice, which is fair enough as long as the choices remain. A decent in-flight meal certainly beats that packet of warm and curling ham and cheese sandwiches stuffed in coat pockets, I guess.

Don't do as I do, do as I say

"Three rashers, three sausages, two eggs, black pudding twice, fried bread twice and no tomatoes," boomed the voice in front of me in the queue. "Oh, and two rounds of toast and a large mug of coffee."

"Beans?" responded the unsmiling automaton in the white overall, a woman with no facial expression whatsoever.

"Goodness no, I'll have wind all day if I do," came the reply.

Wind is the least of your worries, I thought, as I watched the layers of cholesterol being piled onto a very large plate.

I like a cooked breakfast as much as the next person (albeit the vegetarian variety) when I am on holiday, but I know enough about healthy eating to ensure that for most of the year, fresh fruit and muesli is the healthiest way to start my day at home.

"Yes?" snapped the automaton, looking vaguely in my direction.

"Do you have any fresh fruit, apples or bananas maybe?" I enquired hopefully.

"Bananas, no, but you may find some apples in the basket by the till. They may be a bit old though, there's not a lot of call for them in here. I may have got some tinned fruit in the back."

I turned and looked at the two forlorn apples in the basket by the till and decided to give them a miss.

"No, I'll leave that. Just two slices of toast please."

"Do you want them spreading?"

After having seen the thick layer of butter spread upon the previous customer's toast, I declined.

"Do you have some vegetable margarine?"

"Over by the till, but that costs extra."

"Just the toast then, please. No butter."

Whilst I was waiting for the toast, I attempted some conversation. I was curious to know the reasoning behind the massively unhealthy diet being served in the hospital's canteen for visitors.

As with so many hospital facilities in the UK nowadays, the hospital restaurant had been privatised, and I was amused to see it being run by the same company that is involved in school inspections, as well as refuse collections in the UK.

The hospital restaurant was in one of the UK's large city hospitals and I had been visiting an elderly relative in its care.

As is often the case with sick, elderly patients, they can only cope with short visits and so I decided to take a short coffee break before returning to the ward.

"Don't you think it is a little strange that you are serving such unhealthy food in a hospital restaurant?"

"I just does what I'm told. They decides what's to be served," was the snapped response, although now, at least, the face showed some expression and feeling, which was an encouraging development.

"Yes, I can see that, and I'm not blaming you," I protested, "but you are killing your customers. Maybe your previous customer could have been offered a healthier alternative? Surely it's a good opportunity to encourage visitors to consider healthy eating when they visit patients. Maybe some fruit? With a diet like that he'll soon be in here as a patient."

The woman snorted. "He's no visitor," she laughed. "He has that for breakfast most days, and he's a doctor here!"

I ate my toast slowly, with a mixture of disbelief, anger and amusement, but wondering if my elderly relative was receiving the most enlightened care in that hospital after all.

Dentists and Sweet Delights

Most expats will quickly discover that Spanish dentistry is very good. It is mostly private based, with no National Health Service support, and strongly supported by private medical insurance schemes.

There has been considerable investment in dentistry over the years and many young people made dentistry their profession, and this led to a situation where there were too many qualified dentists in the country.

Many newly qualified dentists subsequently moved to other parts of Europe, and particularly to the UK, where they established lucrative practices, and often in areas where there was no dental surgery, and offered treatment under the UK's National Health Service, which came as a relief to many patients.

Over time, dental care in Spain moved full circle and there became a shortage of Spanish dentists working in the country.

This gap was filled with many dentists moving from South America, where Spain has many historical, cultural and trade links, and many dentists from Argentina and Cuba, particularly, established new practices in Spain and the Canary Islands.

I have visited a number of dental surgeries in Spain and the Canary Islands over the years and, with one notable exception with a Swedish dentist in the Costa Blanca, they have all been excellent. New treatments and specialisms are offered in Spain that are often unavailable in the UK.

One example of this is dental implants, which is now becoming more common, yet only two years ago, my dental surgery in the Canary Islands was one of the very few offering this specialist surgery in Spain and much of Europe.

Indeed, it is now possible to have dental implants fitted in one day, and could be part of your holiday in the Canary Islands! Indeed, as with many other medical treatments, such as breast implants and cosmetic surgery, medical tourism is becoming very much part of the new tourist economy of the islands.

Back to the dental surgery business. I am sure that one of the reasons behind the growth of dental businesses in Spain is the Spanish love of sweets! I have rarely seen such emporiums of sweets elsewhere that I see over here.

It certainly puts the old 'Pick and Mix' delights to shame. These sweet shops are usually full of customers, and the large bags of sweets that are carried out of these shops makes me wonder about the health of their teeth.

Most banks, lawyers, accountants, veterinary surgeries, hotels, restaurants and other businesses have a basket of boiled sweets on their counters, or in their waiting rooms, to tempt customers as they pay their bills, or carry out other business. Adults and children alike grab handfuls of these tempting offerings, sucking and chewing as they leave the establishment. My dentist too has a basket of boiled sweets on his counter. No wonder the dental business is doing so well over here!

Expat life, Sport and Community

The
Canary
Islander

Helping Hands

I try to see good things coming out of the bad experiences in life, and good usually defeating evil. Maybe it is all about the fight between good and evil that is often so vividly portrayed in movies, as well as in video games.

Some will possible consider this to be a naive view and take a much more pessimistic view of life. For me, it is not particularly a religious thing, although I do believe that the human experience has to be essentially one of optimism, because without it what would be the point of it all?

We often hear about the 'Wartime Spirit' that prevailed in the UK and other countries during both World Wars, and at other times of national difficulty. Although many of us are too young to remember, it is clear that desperate times often called for desperate measures.

The Canary Islands are not immune from the current financial crisis and many of us have witnessed friends and neighbours losing their jobs, relationships falling apart, and with many returning to their countries of origin.

For the Canary Islanders themselves, times are currently very difficult, with this Spanish autonomous region having one of the highest unemployment statistics in all of Spain.

It is heartbreaking to see so many of last year's school leavers without a job. Many young people are just hanging around with their friends in village and town squares, with little to do and a bleak future ahead of them. What an appalling waste of resources, energy and talent!

Many families, as well as individuals fall through the Spanish Social Security net too. Unlike the UK, there is no automatic right to benefits. There is also the problem of illegal immigrants, with many people not being registered as living on the island.

We may not approve of their illegal entry, but they and their families still have to be fed and cared for. A society that does not look after its weakest members is no society at all.

It was heartening to see a group of ladies collecting food for people in distressed circumstances at my local supermarket last week. As customers entered the store they were simply asked to purchase one additional food item to give to the local charity, which supported the needy in all parts of the island.

The supermarket would then double the quantities of all items purchased from them to help to feed those in need. Items such as flour, rice, pasta, tinned sardines, fruit and vegetables were all items that were welcome. It was good to see so many people giving generously and the collection point outside the store was soon filled with items of generous donations from Saturday shoppers.

I guess this scheme is not unique to the Canary Islands, and I do hope that there are similar ventures operating in all parts of Spain.

As I reached the checkout, the gum chewing, tattooed, teenage checkout girl set about her business of swiping all the items in my basket. She suddenly stopped her work as she saw an elderly and poorly looking woman standing in the queue.

She beckoned her towards the till, but the old lady just nodded and smiled. "No, come over here, you can sit here", insisted the young woman, leaping out of her seat by the till, lowering to the height of the small woman and pushed it towards her. "You sit here and rest." She then stood and resumed swiping the items in my basket.

"That was very kind of you," I commented. The young woman smiled, "Well, we will all be old one day."

I left the store with a warm glow, feeling humbled by the actions of this carefree, gum chewing teenager that I had such brief contact with. I had witnessed many examples of people thinking of others.

Maybe that "Wartime Spirit" that I had heard so much about from my grandfather was not in the past after all.

A Letter from George

A few days ago, I received a letter from an elderly reader, who has occasionally written to me over the years, either to congratulate or to disagree with one of my 'Twitters'.

Although I have never met George, I feel that I know him, as he has told me quite a lot about his life as an expat in Spain, and much of it has been very interesting and, on occasions, very helpful.

I had suspected for some time that George was a habitual complainer and one of the "my glass is half full brigade". Still, it takes all sorts to make an expat world, but I find that a naturally positive outlook is always the best advice for would-be expats.

George, who originated from Preston, had lived and worked in Spain for many years. As is the case with many expats, George had assumed that Spain would be his home for life.

However, suddenly, he had decided to return to the UK for health reasons, as well as intending to resume contact with an ever-diminishing group of family and friends, whom he began to miss even more as he grew older.

The return to the UK was a mistake, and George quickly became disenchanted with the weather, which meant that he had to spend much of his day in a small, cold and expensive apartment.

This, together with the realisation that an adequate pension that had meant a comfortable life in Spain would now hardly pay the essential bills, led George to realise that he had made a grave mistake.

Although he had done his homework thoroughly before moving to Spain some thirty years earlier, he had failed to complete this process in reverse. He was totally unprepared for the many changes that he had to face living in what now seemed a foreign country, and not the "return home" that he had expected.

As George was getting older, he needed his home to be warm, and his first gas bill came as a tremendous shock. He also quickly realised that after living for many years in Spain, his life in the UK, family and friends had moved on.

Some had died, others had moved away, and those who had previously kept in contact a few times a year were busy with their own hectic lives, and they had little time left for George. It was not the homecoming that he had expected, and he began to long for his home, climate and life in Spain.

It was a sad letter, and there were points that helped me to understand some of the many issues that many expats face if they decide to make the return trip to their countries of origin.

George went on to say that he was considering returning to Spain once again; after six months he already had enough of the UK, and this time he was considering moving to Gran Canaria.

He identified the wonderful climate as the main reason, and would I help him to find somewhere suitable to live?

George then went on to tell me that he didn't want to live on either the east or the west coasts of the island. He was opposed to the west of the island, because of the "heavy Atlantic rain" and the strong winds on the east coast.

He was also totally opposed to living in "the fleshpots of the south", because he loathed the tourist industry, and wanted to live well away from tourist beaches and other tourist centres.

As George also suffers badly from travel sickness, he would not wish to live anywhere that involved a journey up a twisting mountain road!

I was now wondering exactly where I could suggest as a new home for George. I briefly considered Las Palmas, but realised that based on other correspondence, George didn't like cities either. Residents of Gran Canaria, and visitors who know the island well, will by now recognise my dilemma.

I wanted to be helpful, but other than Galdar or maybe, Sardina on the north coast, there really was nowhere in Gran Canaria for George to live. Gran Canaria is often called a continent in miniature", and with very good reason, yet I could suggest nowhere really suitable for George.

If any readers do have (polite) suggestions of where they think George would be happy, do please let me know. However, I also suspect that if I did suggest anywhere, George would be the kind of person who would complain for years, and blame me for the suggestion! I give up!

I have come to the conclusion that I will suggest that George moves to Tenerife, and let the good people of Tenerife deal with the problem.

Blisters and sore bums

It is rowing across the Atlantic time again! Why anyone would choose to row across the Atlantic Ocean in a small boat is beyond me, and particularly when there are some very pleasant liners that follow the same route, and with at least three decent meals a day thrown in! I simply don't feel the need to climb a mountain or row across an ocean simply because "It is there."

I do, however, have respect for those who take the view that mountains and oceans have no meaning by themselves and that their very presence inspires a dream of pitting our puny strength against their might, and to conquer not them, but ourselves. Rowers row across the Atlantic for the same reasons that mountaineers climb mountains.

They like a good stiff challenge, and conditions of adversity tend to bring out the best in them. Indeed, it is as much about psychological strength as it is physical.

The Canary Islands are an ideal launching point for east to west ocean rows, being situated at the base of the Trade Wind Belt. It is 3000 miles from the Canaries to the Caribbean.

Although the route begins and ends on islands, it is considered to be a complete Atlantic crossing, and takes advantage of the ideal weather conditions and currents.

December is the time when the races start, and is chosen to coincide with the end of the hurricane season and to get the most benefit from the easterly trade winds and Atlantic currents expected at this time of year.

Rowers who are fortunate to experience favourable current and trade winds can make the trip in as little as two months. Those with bad luck can take three or four months to cover the same distance.

This race follows the most favoured route across the Atlantic seeking the Trade Winds and taking in the warm seas and spectacular wildlife of the mid Atlantic.

Teams from all over the world are attracted to take part in the Atlantic Ocean Rowing Race, which provides ordinary people from a wide variety of ages, abilities and backgrounds with the extraordinary opportunity to take on a once in a lifetime challenge and push themselves beyond their mental and physical limits. For most, it is a life changing experience.

Rowers become all too familiar with extreme temperatures, sore bottoms and blisters, powerful storms, 30-foot waves, non-friendly wildlife and hazardous shipping.

There is no room on board for home comforts, no bathroom facilities, limited cooking ability and a diet of high calorie expedition foods and desalinated water.

Modern rowing boats may not have many amenities, but many are high tech with a wind generator and solar panels to provide power for GPS, reading and navigation lights, radios and the obligatory satellite phone.

Many rowers undertake this challenge as a way of raising money for charity. For me, a soldier who lost both legs in a bomb blast in Iraq and who is to compete the 3,000 mile rowing race across the Atlantic represents the spirit of this competition.

Lieutenant Neil Heritage, from Poole in Dorset (UK) will spend up to 70 days at sea with five crewmembers when he departs from the Canary Islands in December.

Neil will take part in the race without prosthetic limbs and will rely totally on his upper-body strength throughout the race. The six-man team includes four soldiers who were injured in Iraq and Afghanistan.

The men will be raising money for Row2Recovery, a charity that supports servicemen and women wounded in action (further details on my website); I wish them well.

Rowing across the Atlantic may not be for everyone, and neither is climbing Everest. However, for the right person with the right attitude, it could be a dream come true.

Extreme sport or natural selection?

There have been a number of very sad cases recently of mostly British tourists falling off hotel balconies to their deaths in Spain, the Balearic and the Canary Islands.

A recent tragic case of a 22-year-old British man plunging 50ft to his death from the balcony of a holiday apartment in Gran Canaria spurred me on to ask a few more questions about what appears to be a growing phenomena in holiday resorts.

I began to wonder if hotel balconies in Spain, the Balearic and Canary Islands were somehow more dangerous than others. I have stayed in quite a few hotels with balconies in Spain over the years and thought they were no worse than those in Greece, Italy, Portugal or, indeed, the UK.

Maybe ancient hotel and apartment buildings, poorly converted in previous years, were to blame? Maybe they are poorly maintained or lack basic safety features?

It seemed strange that so many of these lethal falls from balconies related to older teenagers and young people in their twenties, yet thankfully very rarely to unsupervised toddlers and very young children, which would be easier to understand in some ways.

Surely, if balconies were so dangerous, there would have been more accidents relating to this younger age group? Yet, I can hardly remember the last time such an accident involving young children occurred in any Spanish resort.

Maybe I was missing something and there were other reasons to be considered, which I had overlooked.

The answer to my questions came in the form of a conversation with a friendly police officer whom I was talking to recently. He drew my attention to another factor that I had never previously considered.

It seems that young, mainly British, holidaymakers when staying in hotels with a swimming pool, have invented a new and dangerous 'sport'. This game is referred to as 'balconing' by the Spanish, and is the name given to a relatively new and dangerous activity.

This new game is usually played by young holidaymakers, who have left their brains behind at Gatwick Airport, encouraged by their friends, and often high on alcohol and drugs, who decide to scramble up the sides of high buildings and then proceed to jump from one balcony to another at hotels and apartments.

Some of the successful attempts are even filmed and proudly displayed on YouTube and other social media sites. Some even deliberately jump from very high hotel balconies in attempts to land in the swimming pool below, rather in the style of Batman, but with much less purpose.

This temporary euphoria often ends in disaster, as the youngsters forget all sense of reality, and as they realise too late that they are not Batman, usually fail to hit the intended spot, and lose their lives, or are permanently injured, as a result.

Young Swedes, Irish and Germans are now also getting in on the act, but it is the Brits who, so far, hold the dubious gold medal in foolishness. In the good old days, it used to be young British men, affectionately referred to worldwide as 'lager louts'.

These lovingly named young people were famed for their binge drinking, colourful language and challenging behaviour. Their charming lack of social awareness and lack of academic prowess made such a fascinating, yet unforgettable impression on holidaymakers in the past.

Now it seems that we have merely moved on to a more modern phase, where some young holidaymakers merely leave holidaymakers with memories of a nasty mess in and around the swimming pool. How very inconsiderate.

Some cultures have rituals and traditions for their young men before they pass into adulthood. These 'rights of passage' are often dangerous, life threatening activities designed to test the strength and 'gene worthiness' of members of the species. It is a process by which the weakest and more intellectually challenged members of the species are weeded out. So is 'balconing' an extreme sport or just a basic form of natural selection?

Look, no lights!

I occasionally hear horror stories from expats, as well as from those who have a holiday home in Spain, who suddenly find that their electricity, telephone or water supply has suddenly been disconnected, without warning and with no reason given.

In some cases, and particularly for those who live in another country and only occasionally visit their holiday home, it is often because their direct debit has been bounced by the bank, because of lack of funds in the bank account.

This is often a simple explanation where maybe there has been some additional expenditure, and overseas bank accounts are infrequently checked and it can be easy to forget to top up an account to meet regular bills for a holiday home in another country.

However, more seriously, I am hearing more frequent occasions when this is not the case. Some friends recently visiting Gran Canaria were shocked to find that on arrival at their holiday apartment, there was no electricity.

There had been sufficient funds in their bank account, yet the direct debit had never been presented to the bank, resulting in disconnection. This situation took several days of their holiday to rectify, and not always easy if you don't happen to speak the language, and in this case involved employing a translator to telephone and later to visit the electricity company.

Eventually, our friends' electricity supply was reconnected, but without the help of the manager of the apartment block, who arranged for a temporary power line to be installed, the first week of a two-week holiday would have been ruined.

We had similar problems with our telephone line with Telefonica some years ago, which was suddenly disconnected for no apparent reason. The bank assured me that there had been sufficient funds in the account, but that no direct debit had been presented.

They also advised me that similar problems had affected other bank customers and suggested that this was during the transition period when Telefonica were in the process of changing their name to Movistar.

Despite considerable argument and representations, Telefonica were totally unsympathetic to the problem, and insisted that I pay a reconnection fee before they restored my telephone line.

As a result, I transferred the line away from 'The Big Beast', as it is often called, to Vodafone, which offered me a much better service, enhanced facilities and at a lower price.

Last week, I became concerned that I had not received or paid an electricity bill for nearly three months. Even though all my essential bills are paid by direct debit, I have learned not to rely upon this and began to fear that I would, like other expats, find myself without electricity.

I checked with my bank, which assured me that no direct debit had been submitted in the last three months.

I called the electricity company and, after several calls, the helpful representative confirmed that it was merely a change in their billing arrangements from monthly to bi-monthly.

Anyway, excuses included August was within the billing period, and little happens in August due to the holidays, and bills are delayed...

The August holiday blip and bi-monthly billing I could understand, but bearing in mind that the change to bi-monthly billing had been announced last year, with the company later reverting to monthly bills a couple of months later, I was totally confused.

The customer support representative finally managed to reassure me that they had once again reverted to bi-monthly billing, confirmed that my account was in order and that I wouldn't be disconnected. However, this still didn't explain the gap of three months in their billing.

As is often the case, all is not always as it seems when living as an expat in a new country, and particularly in August. Fingers crossed that I will keep my electricity supply, but I will let you know what happens if it is disconnected!

Where should I move to?

I often receive emails from readers in different countries telling me of their experiences, or asking for advice. Although I cannot always reply to everyone, I am happy to assist whenever I can. However, one email from a middle-aged couple, Sue and Bill, a few days ago set me thinking.

The email was along the lines of "We know we want to move away from the UK; the Canary Islands sound ideal, so where do you suggest we move to?"

This message was, in many ways, a strange one. Usually, my correspondents know exactly where they want to move to, or who are already there; their questions usually relate to how to make it possible.

This message was different; these writers were completely open-minded, were looking at a blank sheet of paper and could move wherever they wanted to. For me, it was a unique and enviable situation, with the open-minded and fearless attitude common in many idealistic young people, who want to explore the world with only a spare pair of shorts and a toothbrush for company.

My immediate reaction was Gran Canaria, a purely subjective response, of course, because I happen to live here.

Why would I recommend somewhere else? However, I tried to point out that it is always a good idea to visit what would-be expats perceive as their ideal destination first.

The ideal way is during holidays over a number of years, until you begin to feel that a certain place is your second home. Of course, I know this is often not possible.

Emergency situations, illness or a new job may mean that the ideal method of visiting an intended new country over time, and at different times of the year, may not always be possible. Be it the South of France, Slovakia, the Netherlands or the Canary islands, the seasons bring with it different challenges that may either be a delight or an anathema to the intending expat.

So my first piece of advice has to be, try to visit your intended destination at different times of the year and, ideally, over a number of years.

Secondly, different regions of a country, or in my case, the different islands that make up the Canary Islands, are often very different. In the case of the Canary Islands, I adore Gran Canaria because of its 'live and let live' attitude to culture, colour, sexuality, race and religion.

It just doesn't matter what you do, within reason, just as long as it doesn't hurt anyone else.

I am also very fond of Fuerteventura, where we will often take a weekend break. The white sands, brilliant blue sea and an uncompromising landscape always refresh me, as does the very different volcanic landscape of its neighbouring island, Lanzarote.

The smaller western Canary Islands, La Palma, La Gomera, and El Hierro, with their lush forests, small, tight knit communities and lack of modern day facilities is like stepping back in time.

However, could the would-be expat cope without a regular bus service, a decent broadband connection and large well-equipped hospitals to cope with all possible emergencies? I guess what I am trying to say, is that it is 'horses for courses' and you always need to try it out before you commit.

I have known many expats who have sold up in their birth country and immediately purchased a new home in their newly adopted country. This is usually a great mistake, as we all need time to explore and get used to new communities, people and places.

Renting an apartment for a year or two is my best advice. Only then will the newly arrived expat be sure that what was thought to be perfect, really is. If not, it is best move on again, but now just a little wiser.

So, to Sue and Bill, I would also add two further pieces of advice. If you are intending to move to a non-English speaking country, learn the language! Some expats, sadly, never bother, remain in expat enclaves for the remainder of their expat lives and never fully experience the joy of truly living in another country.

Not only should you make an effort to learn the language out of general courtesy to your new neighbours, but in doing so, the door to a new cultural experience opens and genuine expat living begins.

Finally, an essential piece of advice that my first neighbours gave to me when I arrived in Spain, was never believe what you hear in bar gossip or read on some expat blogging sites, where the information given may be selective at best or misleading at worst; always try find out for yourself.

Laws, both local and national, tend to change frequently in Mediterranean countries, and particularly during these times of recession when hard-pressed governments are desperately trying to reign in expenditure.

Invariably, the full facts have often been omitted and some bloggers, in my experience, tend to have a distorted view of cultural, financial and political reality. Bad news and panic make good headlines, and attract many followers, but are rarely completely true.

Try to find out for yourself from a reliable expat newspaper, check with your local consulate, trusted lawyer or new neighbours; they will usually know best, or tell you how to find out.

Christmas

The Poinsettia

This is the time when many Town Halls on the island plant out displays of poinsettia for the festive season. Many roundabouts are planted with a wonderful display of these brilliant red plants.

In the city of Las Palmas, particularly, the display of these cheerful plants, with their bright red foliage and fresh green leaves, make a very attractive and colourful display for the Christmas and New Year season, and last for many weeks.

I enjoy looking at them and remember that when we lived in the UK, we used to buy one for the Christmas season. However, despite my best efforts of careful watering and positioning, after just a few days the plant would drop its leaves, shrivel and die. Over here, they are treated almost as weeds.

The Flor de Pascua, or poinsettia, is an essential part of Christmas in the Canary Islands and they grow wild, mostly on the northern slopes of the island, but are native to Central America.

The Aztecs put the plant to practical, as well as decorative, use and from its bracts they extracted a purplish dye for use in textiles and cosmetics. The milky white sap, today called latex, was made into a preparation to treat fevers.

The poinsettia may have remained a plant native to Mexico for many years had it not been for the efforts of Joel Roberts Poinsett, the son of a French physician.

Poinsett was appointed as the first United States Ambassador to Mexico in 1825. Although Poinsett had attended medical school, his real love was botany.

He maintained his own greenhouses on his South Carolina plantations, and while visiting Mexico he became enchanted by the brilliant red blooms that he saw there. He sent some of the plants back to South Carolina, where he began propagating the plants and sending them to friends and botanical gardens.

The poinsettia is also known by a number of other names including, 'Mexican Flame Leaf', 'Christmas Star' and 'Winter Rose'. My favourite name is 'The Flower of the Holy Night', which has a story that goes like this:

There was once a brother and sister who were very poor, and whose names were Maria and Pablo. At Christmas, parties, festivities and parades were held in the village that excited all the children.

A large Nativity scene was set up in the village church, and all the children were eager to visit the Baby Jesus and to give him a present. Maria and Pablo also wanted to give a present to the Holy Child, but they had no money and had nothing to give.

On Christmas Eve, Maria and Pablo set out for church a little earlier than the others to attend the service. Since they had nothing to give to the child, they picked some weeds from the roadside to make a soft bed for Baby Jesus and to decorate his crib.

While they were still decorating the crib, other children arrived and teased and made fun of them. Maria and Pablo were in tears for their shame and helplessness, but then a miracle occurred.

Suddenly, the weeds burst into bright red petals that looked like stars and were so beautiful that everyone was in awe of their beauty. Everyone then realised that a gift of love is dearer to Jesus than the most expensive presents that money could buy.

I like this story, because it reminds us that expensive gifts are not what Christmas is really about. A Happy Christmas and Festive Season to you all.

Sandcastles at Christmas

I love watching children playing in sand and building sandcastles on the beach. As they grow older, most children quickly become aware that it is only a question of time before the tide comes in, and just one wave destroys all their hard work.

I guess it is experiences such as this that helps children to learn that the joy is in the creation and that nothing lasts forever.

In the Canary Islands, we are fortunate that we can all build sandcastles at any time of the year that we wish, and that the Christmas period is no exception. For me, the Christmas season begins during my visit to the amazing sand sculpture on Las Canteras beach in Las Palmas.

Now in its sixth year, these amazing sculptures are created by a team of international artists at the beginning of December and remain for visitors to enjoy until they are bulldozed away on 8 January.

Thousands of tonnes of sand, water, as well as the skills of eight of the best sand sculpture artists in the world come together to create 'a Belen', a scene that tells the timeless story of the first Christmas.

This year has a particularly interesting and unusual theme, because it merges features of the Canary Islands with Bethlehem, the town where Jesus was born.

Scenes representing Roque Nublo, cliffs, Maspalomas dunes and other aspects of Canarian life co-exist with traditional Bethlehem scenes creating a fascinating and relevant glimpse into Biblical times, which merge with scenes that are so familiar to residents and visitors who know Gran Canaria well.

Artists taking part in this year's 'Arena Bethlehem' are from the Czech Republic, Ireland, Russia, Portugal and Denmark who were given just twenty days to create this year's spectacular scene. Not only does this annual creation help to promote tourism to Gran Canaria, but also adds a very spiritual dimension that is, for many, the start of the Christmas season.

Visitors to the sand sculpture are asked to give a donation, which this year will be given to CARITAS (Catholic agency for overseas aid and development), which operates in 200 countries.

The Christmas season can bring with it so many pressures. Buying and paying for presents, particularly in these troubled financial times, food, drink, and entertaining visitors all take their toll.

Visitors and residents can give the manic Christmas shopping a miss for a couple of hours and take a stroll in the sunshine along Las Canteras beach. There are plenty of traditional bars and restaurants to enjoy and the scenery is spectacular.

These few minutes help people to enjoy and reflect upon the nativity scene created by the hands of these skilful artists and wonder at the story it tells.

Hopefully, the pressures of the Christmas season will begin to ebb away and visitors can begin to enjoy a truly happy and peaceful Christmas.

Roundabouts, Girls and Prickly Cactus

Roundabouts are interesting phenomena in Spain and the Canary Islands. They are a relatively new idea for the country, and it takes time, patience and understanding for most expats to understand the local customs of how to deal with a roundabout.

Most of the locals living near me approach a roundabout as fast as they possibly can, and if anything is likely to hit or obstruct them, they slam on their brakes as hard as possible. Great fun!

I approach a roundabout in the boring, studied way that I was taught, and according to the rules of the British Highway Code, i.e. slowing down, approaching the roundabout with caution etc. Needless to say, the result is that I am usually hooted at in a very aggressive way from the vehicle behind.

Initially, I thought it was because they were admiring my driving skills, but sadly no. Why is it I that too have not learned that roundabouts in Spain are meant to be an exciting daredevil experience of who dares survives the experience?

Have I mentioned the Brits? Well, although the Spanish and Canary Islanders really do take some beating for shear foolhardiness when behind a wheel, British expat drivers really do win the gold medal.

Firstly, they will not accept that it is not normal to drive on the 'wrong' side of the road. By that I mean on the left hand side, when most of the world drives on the right.

Despite many years living in Spain, it is amazing how many British drivers suddenly forget that they are living in Spain, and insist upon driving on the left hand side of the road.

Needless to say, this does tend to cause a few problems for other drivers, and I have witnessed a number of occasions when a car approaches a roundabout at speed, and then proceeds to drive the wrong way around it. It can be a very troubling experience to witness.

When I lived in the Costa Blanca, we had roundabouts adorned with pretty, scantily dressed young women, usually of Eastern European origin, clearly looking for someone to take care of them, offer them warmth and shelter and a cup of soup (this is a family publication, after all!).

After each mayoral election, the roundabout girls would disappear, only to reappear again a few weeks later. A new mayor always meant a temporary slowdown in business, and time for a much-needed break, that's all.

By contrast, roundabouts in the Canary Islands are adorned with spectacular creative masterpieces, real works of art created by local artists and, in the poorer municipalities, many giant prickly, vicious looking cactus.

Yes, you can easily judge the status and wealth of a municipality just by looking at the quality of its roundabouts. It has simply nothing to do with art, but the size of the balance sheet and the influence of the mayor.

A few years ago, our local roundabout was suddenly adorned with a huge and very attractive Christmas tree, appropriately decorated and lit for the Christmas season.

It looked wonderful and, no doubt, added considerable festive pleasure for anyone approaching it. A few evenings before Christmas, a driver headed towards our roundabout and instead of driving around it, decided to head straight for the Christmas tree.

I suspect that he was trying to take his place at the top of the tree. Needless to say, he didn't quite manage it, and the car, driver and Christmas tree were badly injured.

That was the end of Christmas for our roundabout and, since that time, no Christmas tree has appeared during the festive season. Mind you, we do have a wonderful display of prickly cactus, so any drivers considering driving over the roundabout to save time - just beware. Prickly cactus hurt!

Final Thought

Although sending messages in a bottle is a very romantic idea from a bygone age, and could always still be useful, if seriously stranded; nowadays we have much more effective means of communication.

Fax, Emails, text messages, Facebook, Twitter, WhatsApp and iMessage are all new forms of communication that many of us regularly embrace.

What message would you send in a bottle, or by text message, if it could only be a few words?

Maybe it would be your very last words, or just a few words of advice that would make all the difference to the reader in another time and another place…

7818904R00109

Printed in Germany
by Amazon Distribution
GmbH, Leipzig